PLYMOUTH IN TH...

CHRIS ROBINSON

British Library Cataloguing in Publication Data

Chris Robinson
Plymouth in the Seventies

A catalogue record for this book is available from the British Library

ISBN 978-0-9569858-8-0

Written and illustrated by Chris Robinson
Layout Chris Robinson
Cover design Ben Robinson
© Chris Robinson 2015

First published 2015

Published by
Pen & Ink Publishing
34 New Street, Barbican
Plymouth PL1 2NA
Tel: 01752 705337/228120
Fax: 01752 770001
www.chrisrobinson.co.uk

Printed and bound in Great Britain by
Latimer Trend & Company Ltd
Estover Close
Plymouth PL6 7PL
Devon

CONTENTS

1978 aerial view of the City with the Magistrates' Court under construction. Frontispiece: 1979 aerial perspective of Plymouth.

INTRODUCTION

Plymouth in the Seventies, appropriately enough, is the seventh book in the series on Plymouth in the Twentieth Century. Not that they have appeared in chronological order, far from it, but it does now mean that the series now covers the years 1900 to 1980: seven books, with around 1,800 pages and 4,000 images. It's been a true labour of love and hopefully it has brought different time periods to life in a very vivid and evocative way.

Of all of the time periods covered to date, the Seventies is the decade I remember the best. I was fifteen going on sixteen when the Sixties came to a close, so I have been looking forward to covering this decade for some time.

It never ceases to amaze me that so many local historians who try and present an overview of their areas, do so without ever saying much about the time they themselves have lived through.

Richard Worth, who wrote his *History of Plymouth* in the 1890s, had little or nothing to say about the twenty years prior to publication; Plymouth schoolteacher Charles Bracken, writing in the 1930s, devoted just five of his 300 pages on the history of the City to 'Modern Plymouth'; while more recently, Crispin Gill in what is still the best single-volume history of the area, allowed himself just 30 (out of 302) pages to cover the whole of the Second World War and the rebuilding of the city up to the 1990s ... and yet for much of that post-war period he had been Deputy Editor of the *Western Morning News*. He therefore knew most of the main movers and shakers and had first-hand knowledge of the events and circumstances that shaped the City.

What a shame it is that these men shied away so consistently from the period that they could have spoken most authoritatively about.

Not that this book is particularly a critique of the Seventies, rather it is an attempt to try and capture the essence of the decade, to tease out the main stories and illustrate them; and, having collected them all together, present them in a vaguely coherent way.

Hopefully, one day, having covered the more recent decades in a similar way, I will be ready to consider a single volume review of the City's history, but not for a few years yet.

In the meantime, let us consider what the Seventies meant to Plymouth. Of course it's impossible to consider it without looking at the bigger picture. The decade was one of industrial unrest, strikes, demands

New George Street c.1979.

for higher wages, inflation, fuel crises, three-day weeks, and a climate that led to the appointment of the country's first ever female Prime Minister, Margaret Thatcher.

We also had, for the first time, female rugby and football referees, female jockeys, cricket umpires and ball girls at Wimbledon.

Alongside the boundary-pushing liberation front it was also the decade that brought us Ann Summers' Sex Shops, topless models in the *Sun*, naked opera singers on television — Annabel Hunt in Glyndebourne's production of *Ulysses* — while on the top shelf *Penthouse* magazine went pubic.

It was an age of technological advances too as we had the first digital watches, pocket calculators, fax machines, micro computers, in-car cassette players, domestic video cassettes and camcorders, as well as the first generation of home computers.

Many of these machines were beyond the reach of the man in the street, however the disposable razor, the fizzy drink in an aluminium can, the computer tele-tennis game Pong, and the scannable barcode were widespread in no time.

Locally it was a decade that witnessed the demise of freight railway in and out of the City (graphically depicted in Bernard Mills' excellent 'Backtracking' tomes) and a consequential decline in both Sutton Harbour and Millbay as industrial ports.

However, the introduction of the Brittany Ferry terminal to Millbay, as Britain joined the European Economic Community, ensured a degree of ongoing commercial activity around that area.

The Seventies also saw a surge in leisure activities, most conspicuously around the waterfront as first Sutton Harbour and then Ocean Court, at the end of Richmond Walk, were endowed with yachting marinas. Even more significantly, for the economy of the City, the Seventies saw a massive growth in the Further Education provision locally, as the Tech College became a Polytechnic (on 1 January 1970), and the College of Art & Design was relocated into a large, purpose-built premises opposite the Poly. Meanwhile, at Devonport, the old Tech there was incorporated into the brand new College of Further Education, the main part of which was constructed across the road from the old Tech on the former site of King's Road railway station.

The story didn't end there though, for it was in the early Seventies that the College of St Mark and St John completed their move out of London to a site on the northern fringes of the City out by Plymouth Airport and across from the site that had been earmarked for Plymouth's major new hospital at Derriford.

There was major construction work too in the Dockyard, or Devonport Naval Base as it was restyled. Two massive undertakings — the Frigate Complex and the Nuclear Submarine Refit Base — ensured that the defence industry was still to be a significant part of the local economy for the foreseeable future.

Although, having said that, the Royal Navy was the principal beneficiary, as the Army, with the closure of Plumer Barracks and Raglan, and the RAF with the gradual scaling down of Mount Batten, were becoming almost invisible locally.

A situation that was compounded by the activities of the IRA which saw the end of servicemen wearing their uniforms when out and about off duty in the City.

In the City Centre itself, the post-war redevelopment programme rumbled on: in place of the much-loved, Blitz-surviving Drake Circus there appeared Plymouth's first stab at a modern shopping mall. Not quite a fully covered retail offering, it was, nonetheless, welcomed as it brought a few big national names to the City for the first time.

The long-awaited continental clothing chain of C&A was one, and Tesco was another. How eager people were to have these multinationals sucking their surpluses out of the local economy and forcing a number of local independent stores out of business — Costers perhaps being one of the more conspicuous casualties.

Even more so than Ford & Lock, Tesco ushered in the era of the supermarket locally and one by one the City Centre foodhalls of Dingles, Spooners, Littlewoods, British Home Stores … would quietly close.

Socially the Seventies were notable for a host of memorable events, foremost among them the massively hyped Mayflower '70 event at the very dawn of the decade.

This was the event that, it was hoped, would bring vast numbers of visitors to the area, especially Americans. To cope with the anticipated influx two new hotels were built, the biggest in the city to date — the Holiday Inn and the Mayflower Post House — both opened just in time to coincide with the events programmed to commemorate the anniversary of the sailing of the *Mayflower* in 1620.

There was a Massachusetts Week, a Dutch Fortnight, a Drake Week, a 'Come to the USA Fortnight', a cringingly named Keenage Week,

Tavistock Road in the early-Seventies, looking out of Princess House, Drake Circus.

plus an Army Week, an Air Force Week, Royal Navy Week, Young Executive's Week and so on, with hundreds of events listed as taking place between the beginning of May and the end of September.

To say that some of the events in the listings were tenuous in terms of their links to the Mayflower is to understate the situation somewhat.

The opening ceremony was attended by thousands, but enthusiasm waned as the summer progressed. A BBC cameraman filmed many of the highlights, in a film he was to refer to as Mayflop '70. One can only wonder as to how many lessons were learned from that experience.

There were even bigger crowds, however, for some of the other major social events of the Seventies, like the three full houses that Argyle enjoyed, all of which were 'bonus' matches, over and above the normal fixture list.

And so it was that in relatively quick succession we had the visits of Manchester City in the semi-final of the League Cup; Everton in the fourth round of the FA Cup and Santos in a friendly, as the Brazilian side called in on their European tour.

My father, Des, and I were the announcing team at Home Park at the time, along with Douglas Mounce. The atmosphere on each occasion was truly electric and Argyle did themselves proud in every encounter.

In the league, on the other hand, the decade was remarkable mainly for the promotion season under Tony Waiters when Paul Mariner and Billy Rafferty between them scored more goals than the rest of the team put together. How far could we go? With the sale of Rafferty the following season and Mariner the season after that, the answer was not very far at all, and two seasons later we were back in the Third Tier of English football.

But the sporting highlights weren't confined to football. In 1973, partly on account of the Brittany Ferry link opening up our improved connectivity with Europe, the organisers of the Tour de France broke with tradition and, for the first time ever, the famous race, which had been started in 1903, left the Continent. The first stage was held, amid great publicity in the cycling world, in Plymouth, with cyclists doing circuits on the newly opened Plympton Bypass.

Illustrated accounts of all these encounters are to be found in the pages of this overview of Plymouth in the Seventies.

Inevitably, there will be some who read this in the hope that a cherished memory of theirs will be included only to find that it isn't here. Hopefully I have managed to include most things, and certainly more than has ever been covered before, but that is no guarantee that in 250 pages I can do justice to absolutely everything, I only hope that you enjoy what you do read, and will forgive me for any omissions.

Compiling this book has been a privilege and pleasure. It was a joy to look back and recall the people and places that take me back to a decade that had such a big impact on my life.

I left school, went to university, came back, got married and opened a shop on the Barbican. Did I think I'd still have that shop nearly 40 years later? Almost certainly not, but did I even stop to think what I'd be doing in 40 years time … almost certainly not.

But, flicking through the pages of this book I can wind back the clock and smile at the memory of the young man I was then and enjoy revisiting old haunts, finding familiar faces, recalling conversations long forgotten, and now only half-remembered, and wallow in the warmth of the memories.

Chris Robinson *November 2015*

Late Sixties' view of the City Centre with plenty of post-war developments to come in the next few years: including Drake Circus, Plymouth College of Art and Design, and the Money Cent

THE CITY CENTRE

The Swinging Sixties had undoubtedly transformed the nation, but, more specifically, with the construction of the Civic Centre and virtual completion of the first phase of the Post War City Centre re-planning, the decade had made a massive impact on Plymouth.

By the end of the Sixties the House of Fraser had come of age — the building was 18 years-old in 1969 and was one of the cornerstones of the new heart of Plymouth, with its truncated tower mirroring that on the Pearl Assurance Building opposite. The two towers stood either side of the impressive new boulevard that cut through town, from the newly laid out North Cross Roundabout right up to the War Memorial on the Hoe. Together they marked the entrance to the shopping precinct on the northern side of Royal Parade.

By the end of the Sixties that precinct had filled the space west of Old Town Street, north of Royal Parade, east of Western Approach and south of Mayflower Street.

On the north-western end of Mayflower Street there was a great open space that had been earmarked for a mix of retail development and hotel accommodation, while at the top end of Old Town Street another site was being cleared in readiness for a new Drake Circus.

Looking west at Pearl Assurance House down Royal Parade.

As the Seventies dawned, the planting in Armada Way was still in its early stages, only the ancient trees that had formerly stood in Westwell Gardens had reached any significant height.

Meanwhile Guildhall Square was just as Jeffrey Jellicoe had planned it at the start of the Sixties. The Guildhall itself served the city as a major music venue during the Seventies — of which more later.

The 1964 Law Court complex, on the other hand, was proving to be woefully inadequate, particularly after the Crown Courts came here. Hence the decision, in 1972, to move the Magistrates' Courts from here to refurbished accommodation in the former Plumer Barracks at Crownhill.

It was an immensely unpopular decision and was revoked soon afterwards.

Top: *A new zig-zag crossing at the top of Royal Parade.* Above and right: *Princess Square, Armada Way.*

Top: *The 1964 Law Courts, already deemed to be too small.* Above: *The pristine Civic Centre.*

Left: *Guildhall car park — cars 10p.* Above: *Late-Sixties view of Royal Parade at night.*

With new developments still appearing in and around the City Centre, Royal Parade was becoming increasingly busy.

It wasn't just the big red buses — most of them double deckers — that were responsible, it was the increasing numbers of private motor cars and commercial vehicles that had brought new levels of congestion to our cities.

The number of commercial vehicles manufactured in the Sixties was almost as great as that number from the Thirties, Forties and Fifties combined; in fact the number of cars produced in the UK in that same decade, was greater than the total number made, since Frederick

Simms' Daimler first made it's way from Southampton to Malvern, in 1895, right through to 1959.

It was a truly remarkable turn of events and for Royal Parade it meant that this great dual carriageway was increasingly difficult for pedestians to negotiate.

Given that the City's Council Chamber was on the other side of this constant stream of traffic, it was perhaps no great surprise to find that, at the beginning of the Seventies, the Local Authorities decided to ameliorate the situation by creating an underpass right in the middle of the 'gateway' between Dingles and the Pearl Assurance building.

View of Guildhall Square, Royal Parade and Sutton Pool from the Civic Centre.

The work occasioned a great deal of upheaval, and a curtailing of the space available for cars between Dingles and Pearl Assurance, but it certainly made it much easier to get from one side of Royal Parade to the other.

Henceforth the only regular hazard to negotiate was the inevitable busker warbling for coins in the shiny, white-tiled tunnel.

An interesting, but not altogether attractive, rockery greeted emerging pedestrians heading north from the Hoe, while those making the journey in the opposite direction were generally treated to a fine floral display from the City's Parks Department.

The underpass opened in 1973 and, by the summer of the following year, one of the first, if not the first of these displays was a floral celebration of the 100th anniversary of the opening of the Guildhall in 1874.

The new arrangement had the added benefit of making even more of a feature of Plymouth's official flag-post.

The interesting thing about this, incidentally, is that the pole is apparently the point from and to which all mileages to and from Plymouth are measured. Possibly something to do with the fact that the flagpole was located very close to the site of Plymouth's first purpose-built Post Office which stood in Westwell Street before the war.

This page and opposite: *Various shots of construction and completion of the Royal Parade underpass.*

Around the same time as the underpass opened in 1973, Alderman Ralph Morrell announced plans for an exciting new development just to the west of the Civic Centre. The scheme, it was announced, would include a hotel, bars, shops and offices, as well as a concert hall, discotheque and theatre.

The site chosen was that which had been identified in the 1943 Plan for Plymouth as part of the city's new cultural quarter, adjacent to the pre-war Royal Cinema, which stood on the site of Foulston's original Theatre Royal. In 1937 the City Council had sanctioned the demolition of the impressive Georgian structure on the grounds that cinemas were what people wanted then.

Clearly there was still a place for live theatre in the post-war world, but the cheap and cheerful Hoe Theatre - itself an improvement on the Hoe summer marquee — was barely fit for purpose and so the plans for a new theatre were welcomed by many, but not by all. In 1977-78 an anti-theatre group of ratepayers made their feelings known in no uncertain terms. Meanwhile, plans for the new structure were ever-evolving and eventually, after many meetings and a slight reduction in the scale of the proposals, the diggers moved on site and, on 4 April 1979, work began on the construction of Plymouth's new theatre.

Above: *Early designs for the new theatre.* Opposite page: *The site is cleared for the new building and an adjacent car park.*

As the underpass itself bore witness, Armada Way, was, in the Seventies, still a work in progress. Hector Stirling and James Paton Watson's Braille garden had made a significant feature of the top end of the grand boulevard, but much of the rest of the concourse, between the shops, was almost totally featureless. Hence, no doubt, the decision, in the early Seventies, to liven up one or two of these areas with some public art.

Something resembling a very large packet of cigarettes was plonked in the middle of North Cross Roundabout, while just to the north of Mayflower Street there appeared something that looked like a large inverted ice-cream cone with its top lopped. Unsurprisingly perhaps it was called 'The White Koan'.

However it wasn't so much an ice-cream cone that the artist had in mind, rather it was the cones or mounds of white ash that ancient Greeks created in honour of their Goddess of the Hearth — Hestia. Although even that reference was indirect, for the name was evidently a pun on the Buddhist concept of a 'koan' — a device for contemplation, often a puzzling or paradoxical statement.

Described as *'an important sculpture of the early 1970s'* the piece is the work of American-born artist Liliane Lijn. She has made several over the years, this one, I think, is the one now at Warwick University where it went after it's brief visit here in 1972, its year of construction. There is another of Lijn's Koans in the Tate Modern.

Above: Armada Way *with the Money Centre under construction and a new floor being added to Dingles.* Right: *Christmas 1979.*

Above: *Armada Way in 1972, with Liliane Lijn's White Koan.*
Right: *Close-up of the Koan.*

Other intrusions into open spaces in the Seventies included a proliferation of kerbside parking meters, a number of distinctive green-and-cream concrete litter bins and, here and there, the odd weighing machine. A common sight outside chemists and frequently seen at railway — or should that be railweigh-stations — it was common to see them outside chemists.

How many people do you suppose wanted to weigh themselves either before or after having a meal?

Perhaps some were keen to take both measurements, either way it didn't seem all that odd in the Seventies for Stafford Williams and his son Brian to have such a device outside their popular Magnet, Les Routiers-rated restaurant.

It's curious too that it was deemed necessary to flag up the fact that the restaurant was actually licensed, an indication that by no means all of them were in the Seventies. For over 25 years this was a favourite haunt of many Plymothians and the regular venue for many a party or works outing. Stafford and Brian were a rare father and son combination, not only in the restaurant, but also on the board of Plymouth Argyle, while Stafford's conspicuous black Bristol was one of the most instantly recognisable cars around town.

Above: *Stafford William's Magnet Restaurant in Cornwall Street, with its own weighing machine!* Opposite page: *British Home Stores, Armada Way c.1973.*

This page and opposite: *Various views of Frankfort Gate and the Pannier Market.*

Of all the public open spaces in the post-war shopping centre there is only really one that constitutes a 'square' in any sort of formal way, and that is at Frankfort Gate.

The title itself was something of a misnomer as the original Frankfort Gate was much nearer Armada Way; nevertheless it is a gateway of sorts — the Western Gateway into the shopping centre.

With Walls and Pearn's distinctively designed Pannier Market dominating the top end of the square, the north and south side, were the somewhat less inspiring fruits of the City Architect, Hector Stirling's design team. Brick-faced flats occupied the three floors above shop level. The simple 'Easiform' prefabricated affairs brought a bit of contrived colour to the scene, courtesy of brightly painted sections below the windows.

Here we find the only housing that had been introduced into the shopping centre at that time, the City Fathers having consistently refused permission for flats or offices over the shops in the other parts of the post-war centre.

The shop units themselves tended to be smaller than those further into town and consequently there was an interesting array of independents here from the very beginning, with one of the City's first health food shops, Adams' tobacconists, the Stamp Shop and Pete Russell's Hot Record Store, among the retailers looking out over the square.

Above: *1972 view from the Civic Centre. The car parks are almost full and the Culpepper Cattle Co. is showing at the Drake Cinema.*
Opposite page: *King Street railway arch and another view looking down Union Street from the Civic Centre.*

The creation of Frankfort Gate, or more properly Western Approach, had effectively terminated one of the main pre-war arteries into the City Centre.

Indeed, time was when King Street, formerly known as Stonehouse Lane, had been the principal western route into and out of Plymouth from Stonehouse and when the railway arrived, in the first few years of Queen Victoria's reign, there were just two bridges built to carry trains to Millbay above street level.

One was above King Street, the other over Union Street. The damage sustained at Millbay Station put an end to the line's use for passenger trains in 1941, but a goods service continued to operate, on an ever-dwindling basis, for the next 30 years.

In 1971 that service, too, was stopped, rendering the station and the lines to and from it, redundant. One can but wonder how much thought, if any, was given to retaining the route for cars and vans or buses and bicycles.

Certainly not by the journalist Frank Wintle, who described the railway bridge and embankment as *'one of the worst blemishes on the city centre landscape.'*

'Like the Berlin Wall, this bridge divides the City — get rid of it. The Bridge is socially divisive as well.

'Planning experts believe its presence has inhibited investment in Union Street and Stonehouse. Go west of the bridge and you travel beyond the pale. Knock it down and let the bright clean light of the City Centre shine through to Stonehouse.'

If the removal of the railway between Harwell Street and Cecil Street had created a massive opportunity at one end of Western Approach, so too did the closure of Millbay Station and its imminent removal at the other end.

The precise date for the last train journey out of Millbay was Wednesday 30 June 1971. Cyril Champion, a railway employee, made notes at the time. As if aware of its fate, Cyril recorded that the last train scheduled to leave failed just as it got clear of the level crossing out of Millbay and so was allowed to run back under its own momentum. Then the Loco Depot at Laira was called and Diesel 808 was brought down to Millbay to retrieve the stranded engine.

As it pulled clear of the crossing for the second time, Cyril noted that he *'then put all the levers and gates back in the closed position and locked up the box. I walked across the road and entered the Millbay side gate and locked that.'*

And that was that, the last train had left Millbay — it was truly the end of an era.

Quite what the future had in store for the Millbay site was far from clear, but with the imminent removal of the railway lines and connecting bridges it was destined to be very different. Throughout the Seventies, though, this was more or less limbo land.

Opposite page: *10 June 1974 aerial view of Millbay Station.* This page: Top right: *The railway embankment across Union Street and King Street.* Middle: *Millbay Station.* Bottom: *Duke of Cornwall Hotel.* Above: *The last train out of Millbay — 30 June 1971.*

The Union Street bridge was particularly grim. Local resident Alan Clark described it as a no-go area for kids: *'It was like the sin bin of Plymouth. They used to have amusement arcades underneath, when you went down there it was like the gates of doom — even during the day.'*

Before long it was announced that the bridges would indeed come down and that the whole of the Embankment was to be removed.

Before that could happen, however, a number of businesses had to be cleared from under the railway arches in Bath Street and on the other side of the bridge, as well as a few properties that stood on the city side of the bridge. Among them: Plymouth Motor Exchange, Winblack Car Sales, the Auto Snack bar, the Sweet Lemon Café and Wants Second Hand store — where various members of Roxy Music were once spotted trying out guitars prior to their gig in Plymouth Guildhall in 1972.

The much-publicised destructive work attracted a number of rubberneckers and happy snappers, the activity generating more interest than any other demolition job since the original Drake Circus had been pulled down almost a decade earlier.

This page and opposite: Various views of the doomed bridge over Union Street, before and during demolition. Note in the top right image Capstan cigarettes are being advertised at 20p a packet.

Crowds assembled, the road was closed and one by one the thirty great ten-ton steel girders were removed from the structure that had carried stars like Bing Crosby, Walt Disney, Cary Grant, Charlie Chaplin, and Gracie Fields across Union Street, en route for London from Millbay. Plymouth's liner trade had long since gone into decline by 1974, when the bridge disappeared after 125 years of service, nevertheless, it was a significant moment in the city's history. The removal of the bridges and the embankment not only altered the immediate appearance of the area, lightening the whole space, but it also created a massive site, ripe for development. The big questions were — what would be built on the newly created open spaces, and how long would it be before that happened?

This page and opposite: *Going, going, gone — the Union Street bridge comes down and the divide between the City Centre and Stonehouse is removed.*

Whatever was to happen, Union Street was no longer a street of two halves, although clearly everything that was east of Western Approach was post-war, while almost everything to the west, at that stage, was pre-war.

Plans were afoot to change the old part of that famous thoroughfare in a major way, however, and, now that the bridge had gone, work soon began on clearing the western end so that the whole stretch from Western Approach to Stonehouse Bridge could be made into a dual carriageway, just as the short section of Union Street between Derry's Cross Roundabout and the Prince Regent was already.

Throughout the Seventies work was carried out towards that end and, one by one, pubs, shops and other premises that lined the street — beyond the Palace Theatre, were cleared. Ultimately, however, the Palace held the key and the fact that it achieved listed status meant that the dual carriageway was no longer feasible.

Meanwhile, back at the Derry's Cross end of the street, the Co-op was at the heart of life at the bottom end of town.

Well known for their readiness to embrace Christmas with a major external display, they also rose to the Mayflower '70 challenge with a massive representation of the Pilgrim's ship that hung down a whole two storeys from their top-floor balcony.

Left: *The path is cleared.* Above: *TSB, Derry's Cross.*

Above: *Co-operative House in Mayflower '70 mode.* Top: *Bargain hunters on Sale Day.*
Right: *Derry's Cross Roundabout.*

This book when completed and exchanged for goods is worth **£1**

CO-OP

Exchange it in the departments specified by your Society

Although still a separate and distinct body within the Co-operative movement, the Plymouth & South Devon Co-operative Society was gradually buying into the national movement's branding initiatives — although perhaps not quickly enough to halt the inexorable rise of the privately owned supermarkets.

In 1968 they had adopted the new 'clover leaf' Co-op logo and in February 1970 they joined the National Dividend Stamp Scheme. The scheme had been launched around the time that the new logo had been unveiled and was a belated response to Tesco's championing of the Green Shield stamp phenomenon that had been introduced to Britain, from America, ten years earlier.

Clearly, it was an easy model for the Co-op to adopt as the tool was tailor-made for their existing dividend scheme. Henceforth, stamps were issued at the rate of two for every shilling spent. The little pale blue, lick and stick stamps were entered into a pocket-sized book which, when full, had a cash value of ten shillings for Co-op members, but only eight shillings for non members.

A year later, however, such sums had been rendered meaningless as 15 February 1971 saw Britain go decimal as the old LSD (librae, solidi, denarii — pounds, shilling and pence) system, whereby there were 240 pennies to the pound, was replaced by the new 100 pence to the pound.

To help ease their customers through the process, and allay fears of unwarranted price increases off the back of the move, the local Co-operative held help tutorials and hired a caravan to go around tthe estates to explain exactly how it all worked. They also created some impressive window displays showcasing the new coinage alongside the latest fashions.

Opposite page and this page: The Co-operative Society do their bit to guide customers through the decimalisation process, with window displays, lectures and a touring van.

Above and right: *New George Street.* Far right: *Front page of the Herald, which, like Costers, was based in New George Street.*

West of Armada Way, the Co-op was unique in having entrances off Royal Parade and New George Street.

Meanwhile, at the dawn of the Seventies, Lawson's were probably unique in having business premises on either side of New George Street — one just below the entrance to the Pannier Market, the other adjacent to the offices of the *Western Evening Herald* and *Western Morning News*.

However, the situation didn't last long into the new decade. On 1 January 1971, John Lawson formally took control of the family firm and, after a thorough review of the business, decided to close the Garden Shop at the bottom end of the street and focus on their main outlet. The decision was accompanied by significant re-investment in the latter, investment that saw the shop-front extended and a large marble fascia appear below David Kindersley's strikingly effective stone-etched 'Lawson' sign.

The new arrangement won an additional 400 sq.ft. of floor space and prompted a serious reconfiguration of the internal layout. Cutlery was moved to mezzanine, the garden department moved to front of house and most significantly of all, two new checkout points were installed towards the doors.

'One of the problems with our previous arrangement with a till on each counter was that someone needing quite a bit of service and advice could hold up a number of people who had found what they needed and simply wanted to pay and leave,' said Mr Lawson, who was keen to emphasise that the new arrangement would not impact on service.

Lawson's were a long-standing Plymouth firm and had been in the street since 1904 (originally in the pre-war Frankfort Street), so too had Costers, another family run concern. However, in October 1978, their managing director announced that Costers were closing. *'We are too big to be small and not big enough to be big,'* reasoned Geoffrey Leatherby. *'We have not got the buying potential to compete with the big chain companies all around us, neither have we the steady flow of capital to inject into the company to refurbish and up-date our image.'*

Sadly the closure meant the loss of 70 jobs, but the good news for this part of town was that the new occupiers of the Coster's building were going to be WH Smiths, for whom this would become their largest outlet in the South West.

Above: *Lawsons, next door to the* Herald *and Morning News Offices, undergoes a transformation.*

Above: *Royal Parade from the bottom and from the top. The No.14 service to Keyham was withdrawn in the late Seventies — this shot is probably Spring 1973.*

Another long-established local firm on the move in the Seventies was W Mumford the motor firm that had been started by William Mumford at the beginning of the twentieth century.

William had broken away from his father's carriage-making enterprise in 1900 and had set up stall in Ebrington Street. Subsequent expansion saw them establish a showroom and engineering works in Salisbury Road in the 1920s and then, in the 1930s, a major new complex in St Andrew Street. That facility, in turn, closed in the late-1970s and the next step saw them relocate to a new '£100,000 development at Crabtree Roundabout'.

That original move to St Andrew Street had occasioned the demolition of a number of truly ancient properties below Abbey Place — in what is, after all, one of the oldest streets in Plymouth. Happily, the street survived the war pretty much intact; however, no sooner had Mumfords moved out than the garage building was demolished to make way for Plymouth's bright new Magistrates' Court. The courts had previously been held in the 1960's law court complex off Armada Way, but the decision to move the Crown Courts there had put pressure on that site and the Magistrates were relocated to Crownhill.

The inconvenience of that arrangement was swiftly vocalised and the St Andrew Street site was ultimately deemed to be the best solution, notwithstanding the fact that it would totally compromise one of the major routes from the City Centre to the Hoe and the Barbican.

In the event, the new Magistrates' Court was opened here in 1979 by Prince Charles. Designed by Tony Irish, it was the first purpose-built Magistrates' Court in Plymouth and a great deal of the internal arrangements and layout were influenced by the then Clerk to the Magistrates, Cliff Moiser.

Marvellous as the new facility was deemed to be, it nevertheless cut St Andrew Street in two and totally blocked any view of the recently restored Tudor building that stood in the bottom half of the thoroughfare. Said to have been the home of James Parker, a celebrated Elizabethan sea captain, merchant and Mayor of Plymouth, the building was fully restored by the City Council, between 1972 and 1977. Thanks largely to the energy and enthusiasm of the City Museum and Art Gallery Curator, James Barber. However, even his passion for the history of the area couldn't prevent the construction of the Magistrates' Court and the demolition of yet more properties in the bottom half of the street, further isolating the Merchant's House.

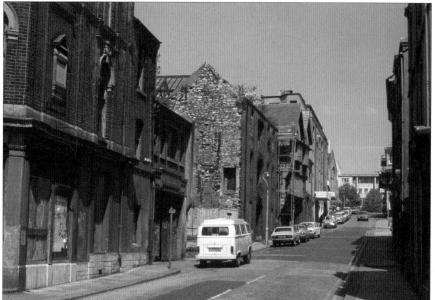

This page: *St Andrew Street evolves in the Seventies as Mumford's move out, and the Magistrates' Court is built across the site. Meanwhile, the bottom end is cleared below the restored Merchant's House, which is opened to the public as part of the Museum service.*

If any Plymouth building could be said to have been isolated by the post-war redevelopment of the City, though, it was Charles Church. Like the Merchant's House it had stood through the Civil War and the Second World War, Charles Church was, sensitively and significantly, left as a shell after the Blitz of Plymouth, to serve as a reminder of the horrors of war and as a memorial to the civilian war-dead of the city.

However, where once it had been at the hub of a busy, built-up area, now it stood in the middle of a roundabout, in a sparsely populated part of town, with no pedestrian access of any kind.

Although the construction of Bretonside Bus Station had started that process in the late-Fifties, and the erection of the area's first self-service petrol station, Turnbull's, had added to that island status in the early-Sixties, the Seventies saw yet further steps taken along that path.

There was the new Drake Circus shopping centre on the north western perimeter; a new Art College and a new Police Headquarters on the northern side; plus, just to the east of that, there was a major curtailment of that end of Ebrington Street. The street had at one time reached as far west as Old Town Street, now it ended just above the Victorian Green Street Almshouses.

This latter exercise involved the demolition of the fondly remembered Ham Street Vaults.

Last orders were called here on 28 October 1972 and three weeks later bulldozers made sure there would no further drinking-up time.

Right, top: *Exeter Street viaduct c.1973.* Bottom: *The viaduct in the late-Sixties with the doomed Ham Street Vaults (above) still visible.*

With no shortage of activity above Bretonside in the Seventies, there was a fair degree of hustle and bustle in the bus station itself.

While car ownership was having an undoubted impact on bus usage and the coach-outing, day-tripper market and cheap package holidays were affecting longer tour travel, the Seventies were still relatively prosperous for tour operators.

The Beeching cuts to the national rail services in the Sixties had driven an increase in coach travel, as had the slightly earlier (1961) decision to allow coaches to travel at 40mph, rather than just 30mph.

In 1968 a new Transport Act saw the nationalisation of private bus and coach services and brought about the creation of the National Bus Company the following year. Before long this would be re-branded as National Travel and soon after that, National Express.

Meanwhile, the locally operated Embankment Coach Company teamed up with the Leeds-based Wallace Arnold ... a firm that had been founded by Wallace Cunningham and Arnold Crowe shortly before the Great War in 1912.

By the end of the Seventies, operating under the Euroways banner, the company were responsible for taking thousands of UK holiday-makers to the Continent.

Much closer to home, back in Plymouth, the City was still promoting itself as the 'Centre of 100 Tours' and it was never a surprise to see Bretonside Bus Station filled with chrome-lined, facility-free, seatbelt-less but comfy coaches.

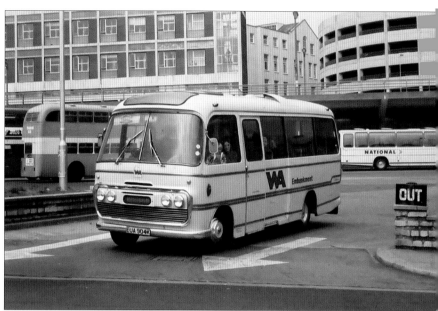

Above: Bretonside in the sun c.1968. Top right: Wallace Arnold Embankment Coach leaving Bretonside April 1974. Middle and bottom: Bretonside interior and exterior, 1971.

The capacity of Bretonside bus and coach station was rarely, if ever, completely stretched. By contrast, the demand for private car parking in the City Centre often exceeded availability. The issue, therefore, was one that the local authority were wary of when it came to planning the size and scale of the car park, designed to service the new Drake Circus complex, that sprang up at the beginning of the Seventies.

Built for the Laing Development Company, in association with Plymouth City Council, the project ultimately led to the construction of one of the oddest and probably the ugliest Seventies' structures to be seen in the City — the Drake Circus car park.

Remembered mostly for the dizzying spiral ramp-way that all vehicles had to use to exit the premises, it looked rather more like the skeleton of a building, than a finished piece of architecture, and that, it would appear, is exactly what it was. The story seems to be that when the City's engineers took their plans for the car park to their masters, they were duly informed that the cost of the proposals exceeded the budget. Thus the engineers were instructed to take a complete floor off the scheme, and return with fresh proposals.

This they did. However, it was not just an easy matter of Tippexing the top storey and representing the drawings with one floor whited out. The stresses and strains of building one less floor required recalculating the project from the beginning. And so, it seems that when the engineers went back with revised figures they had good news and bad news for their masters. The good news was that they had done as instructed and designed a building with one floor less. The bad news was that because ten months had now passed since the first set of drawings had been presented, the level of inflation then affecting material and labour costs meant that it was going to cost the same sort of amount as it would have done in the first place, with the extra floor.

Thus it was that the engineers were instructed to cut costs, at all costs, and in the end that meant creating the bare bones of a building with none of the softening superstructure that might have rendered it just that little bit more aesthetically acceptable.

Above: *The vertebrae of the skeletal Drake Circus car park. Opposite page: Views of Exeter Street, east of Charles Church, with the Jubilee and Burton Boys pubs, neither of which were long for this world.*

One of the inevitable impacts of increasing the amount of traffic looking to come into the City Centre was that it put great pressure on the main roads carrying that traffic in and out.
It was, therefore, no surprise to find that there were plans to widen Exeter Street between Charles Church Roundabout and Cattedown Roundabout. Sadly that meant that there was no point in making long-term plans for two of the well-known pubs that lined that route, the Jubilee and Burton Boys, corner pubs at the end of the junction with Sutton Road.

Meanwhile, heading towards the northern route out of the City, there was plenty of activity on both sides of the newly laid out Charles Street. While Drake Circus shopping mall and car park were under construction, on the bottom side of the dual-carriageway, the Art College, swiftly followed by the Charles Cross Police Station, were being built on the upper side.

Of all of these developments Drake Circus had the largest footprint and was the most eagerly anticipated. Apart from the Pannier Market, Plymouth had no real sheltered shopping mall where a variety of stores could be accessed without getting wet if it was raining, and with one of the highest rainfalls of any city in the country, that could be quite often. However, in the event, while the new shopping complex was undeniably traffic-free and pedestrian-friendly, it was, notwithstanding the canopies, quite open to the elements. Furthermore, there was no real rainproof route to the multi-storey car park and so it didn't perhaps get the rapturous warm welcome it might have done.

It did, however, mean that the much longed-for arrival of C&A, the Dutch textile company founded by brothers C & A (Clemens and August) Brenninkmeiger had at last come to Plymouth, some 50 years after opening their first store in England.

The new shopping precinct also included Plymouth's first Tesco store, complete with its own in-house bakery, generating enticing odours that wafted gently across the upper level of the concourse.

Top: The new Plymouth College of Art & Design takes shape.
Right: The site is cleared and a new, and much bigger, Drake Circus appears on the site of the old one.

Late-Seventies aerial view of the City Centre eastern end.

47

Drake Circus wasn't just the domain of the chain stores though, as an eclectic mix of retailers occupied units that ranged massively in shape and size.

Pet food, fruit and veg, buttons, bows and beads, toys, games and stationery were all available here.

Furthermore, the Drake Circus development was always more than just a new shopping centre: it also came complete with a five-storey office block — Princess House.

This spectacularly uninspiring oblong box never seemed to be fully let, although that may not have always been the case. Multinational financial services company Legal & General occupied a considerable part of the building, but there appeared to be massive 'To Let' signs across one floor or another much of the time.

Above: The underpass leading into Drake Circus from the Polytechnic. Right: The main route through the upper level. Opposite page: Princess House office block at Drake Circus.

This page and opposite: *Stephen Johnson and fellow Art College students mimicking mannequins in Drake Circus, note both Tesco and John Conway were offering Green Shield stamps. Opposite bottom: Plymouth's only ever outdoor escalator and ads for John Conway and the Chapter and Verse bookshop.*

One of the quirkier attractions, when it was working, of the new shopping centre, was the open-air escalator which ran down from the front of the Arcadia Newsagents on the corner of what almost constituted a square in the middle of the upper level. Just around from them, on the inside corner was the rather wonderful Chapter & Verse bookshop.

Occupying a prime corner site opposite Arcadia on one side and Tesco on the other, was, for a while, John Conway menswear. Advertising themselves as the main stockists, locally, for Levi, Wrangler and Lee jeans. They attracted large numbers of young people who enjoyed a greater level of spending power than their parents or grandparents before them.

The firm, which had become an incorporated company in Plymouth during the war (December 1941) and had branches in Exeter and Torquay, also, at the time, offered Green Shield stamps with all purchases. Targeting the even younger customer, there was a Special Double Green Shield stamp school discount available, or a more simple 5p in the pound discount.

It's interesting that the Green Shield stamp phenomenon had been popularised in this country after its adoption by Jack Cohen (the 'co' element of Tesco, the company he had founded back in the 1920s). The stamp idea had actually been introduced into the UK from America, by a London printer, Richard Tompkins, who noticed how popular the scheme was when he was on holiday in Chicago in the late-Fifties.

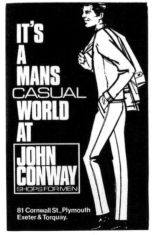

IT'S A MANS CASUAL WORLD AT JOHN CONWAY
SHOPS FOR MEN

81 Cornwall St., Plymouth
Exeter & Torquay.

LEVI'S

Great casual trousers that keep their good looks.
Washable and non-iron.

An exciting new fabric with a sheen.

Elegant slant pockets.

Creases that stay.

Young-style straight leg.

Sta-Prest trousers from the Levi's people

JOHN CONWAY

Drake Circus & Cornwall St. Plymouth
Special School Discount of 5p in the £ or
Double Green Shield Stamps

This page and opposite: *A very Seventies opening for Jon Saberton's new outlet in DC — Drake Circus — pretty girls, big wigs. beach buggy and high fashion.*

Another Plymouth fashion retailer who opened a unit in the new development was Jon Saberton. With a slightly more exclusive flavour, Jon had opened his first outlet in a unit in Mayflower Street, in November 1963, when that stretch was newly built, and now here he was, eight years on, looking for the higher footfall that the Drake Circus development promised. Curiously enough, the section that ran east-west along the line of what had been Ebrington Street was rechristened Eastlake Street, in honour of the celebrated local artist, Charles Locke Eastlake, who famously painted Napoleon when the latter was in Plymouth Sound, a prisoner on board the *Bellerophon*. Meanwhile the upper, traffic-free, pedestrian route that backed on to the premises on the north side of Eastlake Street, was given the address of Eastlake Walk.

Other businesses in the complex included Ladybird, Myrna's, Kendall and Ravel's shoe shop.

53

Overall, the new Drake Circus added to the City's retail offer and enabled the tourist brochure copy writers to boast that, *'as a shopping centre, Plymouth is now the largest and finest between Bristol and Land's End, with the most comprehensive range of shops in the South West.*

'So important has this shopping area become that every store and fashion house worthy of the name has seen fit to open a branch here alongside shops whose names have been a Plymouth tradition for many decades.'

However, local names were increasingly becoming the exception rather than the rule. In the same year that Drake Circus opened, Dingles department store became part of the House of Fraser group, meanwhile, six years later, in 1977, John Yeo's and Spooners were renamed Debenhams: this was something of a formality, as it happened as Debenhams had actually taken over Spooners back in the 1920s and Yeo's in 1964. Nevertheless, it was an indication of the ever-increasing homogenisation of the high street.

A situation that was compounded by the fact that other long-standing local firms, like Tozers and Costers, were both forced to call it a day.

This page: *External views of the new Drake Circus development opened by Princess Anne on 17 November 1971. The scheme was built for the Laing Development Company in association with Plymouth City Council.*

Above: *Twilight shopping in the new Drake Circus. The barriers were a poor solution to random pedestrian crossing issues.*
Left: *View looking down Old Town Street from Drake Circus.*

Just across from Drake Circus there was another Seventies development, but at the other end of the decade. A striking, clean-lined structure that looked a little like a Lego building, it stood guard at the entrance to Mayflower Street and housed the offices of Western Trust and Savings. Handy for the neighbouring Good Companions pub, which itself had only just opened in 1969. The office employees also had a new Greek restaurant, Zorro's at their convenient disposal, in the adjacent and integrated structure on the southern side of the building.

Plot by plot, post-war Plymouth was gradually being populated by new developments but there was still a curious little group of pre-war properties, the remnants of Rowe Street, that looked out over Princess House and the new roundabout with its lengthy subways, that connected the various locations.

It was in one of these properties, in the mid-Seventies, that John Baldwin started his jewellery business.

Top: *Late-Sixties view along Cobourg Street and Mayflower Street.* Above: *The new Money Centre.* Opposite page: *Aerial view of the same area taken c.1979.*

Another relatively new business in the area was the Polytechnic Bookshop in Mayflower Street. Opened just in time for Christmas, in December 1966, the bookshop was the brainchild of Leslie F Paul, a former Lord Mayor of Plymouth and proprietor of the newspaper wholesale business started by his father, Louis Paul, in Union Street, in 1894.

Leslie's daughter, Lorna, and her husband, Michael Sewell, were responsible for the running of the establishment, Michael taking on the management role in 1971 when Lorna went to run the wholesale side of things.

Oddly enough, Plymouth didn't officially have a Polytechnic in 1966, just a College of Technology, but the designation had been anticipated since Tony Crossland's White Paper appeared earlier that year and eventually came into being on 1 January 1970.

Allen's Garage in Cobourg Street also occupied quite contemporary premises: as the City's Vauxhall dealers, the poignancy of the 1979 batch of Vauxhall Vivas was possibly missed at the time but they turned out to be the last solely Vauxhall-designed passenger car produced. All subsequent models would be badge-engineered Opel vehicles.

This page: Allen's salesman Roger Harcom, outside the firm's Cobourg Street premises with the latest, and last, Vauxhall Viva in production, ready for the Lord Mayor's Day Show. Opposite page: The Polytechnic Bookshop in Mayflower Street, with some of the decade's big sellers.

The late-Sixties had seen massive changes in the Cobourg Street area: many of the pre-war buildings there had survived the war but were cleared away as part of the work needed to create a dual-carriageway around the top end of town.

Western Approach, particularly in the wake of the removal of the railway leading into and out of Millbay, was, similarly, a work in progress for much of the Seventies.

The situation was compounded towards the end of the decade when plans were announced to create a new inner-city school on the eastern side of Oxford Street.

The grand limestone pile that was Oxford Street Primary School had been opened in 1880 by the then Mayor of Plymouth, William Derry, he of the clock tower fame, and might still be standing now, had not its headmaster, John Pugh, been put in an unenviable position.

The school lacked a proper playground and had little or no greenery to soften its surroundings. Mr Pugh was told he could have a new school, with plenty of surrounding play areas and green spaces, as long as he was prepared to accept the demolition of the old building. There was, he was told, no possibility of the old school remaining and new facilities being created for it. The only way he could get a valuable space for his children to play, plant and grow things, was to agree to have an all-new development: single storey buildings on a much bigger footprint.

Thinking primarily of the children he agreed. Of course, in order to create such an open space in such a built-up area, dozens of houses, a handful of shops and notable other premises, like Furguson's old fizzy drinks establishment, had to be sacrificed.

This page: *Selection of images taken by Oxford Street Primary teacher Keith Loze before the site was cleared to create a new school for the area — Pilgrim Primary.* Top: *Corner of Cambridge Street and Oxford Place.* Middle: *Mineral works.* Bottom: *Cambridge Street.* Above: *The view across Western Approach before demolition.*

Above: *Bernard Mills' shot of the top of Saltash Road, near North Road Station, June 1970.*
Left: *Tracey Street.*

The last remaining vestiges of King Gardens, Cambridge Lane West and Cambridge Street were cleared away in the process. It was a bitter sweet moment for many:

'Oxford Street is old and grey.
How old it is,' people say.
But alas the day is nigh,
When Oxford Street will say "Goodbye",
In the sadness and in the gloom,
A kind of happiness will begin to bloom.
Because we'll have a brand new school.
With gardens and a swimming pool.'

So wrote Helen Demeranville, a pupil at the school, at the time the children prepared to move out of their old home.
This was a part of Plymouth that had been dubbed 'New Town' when the area was first developed from the 1820s onwards; now it was undergoing its first major transformation in a hundred years, with apparently not too much heartache.

Top: *Oxford Street Primary playground.* Above: *Warsol's with All Saints Church, Harwell Street.* Above right: *Bottom of Ilbert Street, Betty Swan and her husband ran the general shop that the Oxford Street children called the Tuck Shop.* Opposite page: *Oxford Street Primary School.*

Such is not to say that there had not been odd pockets of redevelopment prior to the Oxford Street School upheaval.

New flats had already been built in Claremont Street and the modest former Victorian beer house, the Valletort, that had stood towards the bottom end, had been entirely rebuilt.

Albert (Bob) Trotter was the colourful landlord there throughout the Seventies.

At that time there were a number of properties in the area that were in need of either replacement or significant repair. One Oxford Street teacher recalled visiting a family in Well Street.

'The family had three children, but only one cold tap, strung across the main living room on a hose and a piece of string.

They had been rehoused when their previous property in Brunswick Terrace had been compulsorily purchased as part of the road-widening of Exeter Street. The Well Street property had few facilities, no carpets and the windows were boarded up.

'It's hard to imagine families living in worse conditions before the war: the house was squalid and very smelly, as were the family, but, under the circumstances, it was easy to see why.'

Well Street and Harwell Street were ripe for redevelopment.

Top: *The Valletort.* Above: *Valerie Durham's car is one of the few vehicles parked in Ilbert Street, looking towards North Road West.* Right: *Well Street.*

Above: *May 1977, the No.27 bus, in Jubilee livery, travels east on North Road.*
Inset top: *No Place Inn, at the end of North Road West.* Inset left: *North Road West.*

Hotham Place.

Somewhat older than the properties around the former New Town, were the houses that once lined the northern bank of Stonehouse Creek. One of the City's more distinctive terraces, these have tended to attract those more inclined to restore, than to refashion, and to maintain, rather than neglect.

In the 1890s the upper stretch of the creek, above Millbridge, had been filled in to form Victoria Park: a deliberate attempt to create a play area for the young men of Plymouth, and to keep them away from the Hoe which was fast becoming an area set aside for tourists and, therefore, one the authorities wanted to keep potential ruffians away from. In the 1970s, it was the turn of the lower stretch of the creek, below Millbridge, to be infilled, partly as a response to complaints about the smells generated at low tide and partly to create playing fields for Devonport High School for Boys and Tamar School, which in the Seventies started to admit girls for the first time.

Meanwhile, a little beyond the bridge, on the Stoke side, two pubs serviced the area, with one, the Millbridge, garnering a formidable reputation throughout the Seventies as one of the best pub jazz venues in the South West. Landlord Jack Mitchell regularly booking local favourites like the Climax Jazz Band, the Banjo Bone Band and Hefty Jazz, with local star Rod Mason making regular guest appearances.

Top left: *Millbridge pub sign*. Top: *The Edgcumbe*. Above: An entrance to *Victoria Park*.

THE BARBICAN

The Barbican was still very much a working harbour as the Seventies dawned, with the fishing industry conveying a general air of activity around Sutton Harbour.

However, although there were a healthy number of vessels still unloading at the grand, Victorian, railway-styled fish market, there was a gradual decline in the commercial operations taking place elsewhere around the pool.

The closure of the Coxside coal-based works in 1969, following on from the establishment of the 'ultra modern', 'gas-from-oil' plant at the Breakwater Works at Oreston, saw a massive dip in the fortunes of the coal wharf to the side of East Pier.

The subsequent introduction of a commercial ferry service from Brittany into Millbay in 1973, followed by a second, from Santander, in 1978, further contributed to the decline in overall tonnage in and out of Sutton Harbour, and by the end of the decade, the port's days as a mercantile shipping centre were clearly numbered.

Opposite page: *Late-Seventies view of Plymouth.*
Above: *Marquand Brothers fruit wholesalers operating out of Looe Street*

The Kathleen & May, *moored in Sutton Harbour for most of the Seventies.*

Serving almost as a wistful reminder of those heady days of the past, 1971 saw the arrival of the *Kathleen & May* in Sutton Pool.

Launched as the *Lizzie May* in April 1900 from the little Welsh port of Connah's Quay, the *Kathleen & May* (she was renamed in 1908) spent her early years as a light cargo boat.

Passing down through a variety of hands over the years, the *Kathleen & May* was destined to become the first boat to be acquired by the newly formed Maritime Trust founded by the Duke of Edinburgh.

Refitted at Mashford's Yard, Cremyll, with further financial assistance coming from Sir Yue-Kong Pao and World Wide Shipping, Hong Kong, the celebrated schooner was first opened to the public in Millbay Docks, but was moved to a mooring alongside the Three Crowns, in the hope of attracting greater visitor numbers.

Here the numbers were better but not good enough and in 1978 she was moved again, this time to the newly restored Victorian Dock, St Catherine's in London.

Top right: *The* Kathleen & May. Inset: *The Duke of Edinburgh inspects the vessel.*
Above: *Looking across to Vauxhall Quay.*

Curiously enough, visitor numbers to the Barbican generally improved throughout the Seventies. Plymouth Gin, in Southside Street, was offering the occasional tour, while the Refectory Room, which had been restored and re-opened in the early-Sixties, was regularly listed as one of Plymouth's main attractions. More often than not, off the back of the claim that it was reputedly *'the final meeting place of the Pilgrim Fathers prior to sailing to America in 1620'*.

Undoubtedly one of the oldest buildings in Plymouth, and possibly the town's first guildhall, the claim is quite feasible. Less likely, if not downright false, is the longstanding suggestion that the building was part of a Black Friars establishment, although it is possible that stonework from the neighbouring Grey Friars monastery, in New Street, was used in the construction of parts of the property.

Alcohol had long been allied to the attraction of the Barbican area and in the Seventies that relationship was enhanced in a number of ways, not least of which was by the opening of two new wine bars within days of each other.

A whole host of wine bars had sprung up in the early-Seventies in London, spearheaded by Julia Carpenter's Wolsey Wine Bar chain — she opened 15 in one year! Taking the place of the ailing, low-profit-margin coffee bars, which had had their heyday in the late-Fifties, early-Sixties, wine bars were, for many, a welcome alternative to pubs and offered women a comfortable and respectable venue for a lunchtime drink and nibble.

John Dudley, who would, before the decade was out, establish Cap'n Jaspers outdoor eatery at the entrance to the Fish Market, had already brought the idea to Devon. Having set up Dudley's Wine Bar in Kingsbridge, he applied for a licence to bring a similar concept to Southside Street. On the very same day, an old school-friend of his, Cedric (Ziggy) Talbot-Weiss, applied to do the same, in an ancient, and formerly waterside, warehouse in Quay Road, which runs parallel to Southside Street.

In the event, Dudley's and Oysters (as the other one was initially known) both opened in June 1975 and were well-received.

Despite these developments, Southside Street, at that time, still operated as a kind of village community hub, with many of the shops you would expect to find in such a centre, including a chemist and a post office; however, changes were coming as the increasing numbers of visitors ushered in a fresh culture to this historic quarter.

Opposite page: *Southside Street.* Inset: *A tour of Plymouth Gin.*
Top right: *Plymouth Gin Distillery and Wood's Chemist.* Bottom: *Southside Street with a Post Office on the corner of White Lane.*

Top: *Robert with his nearly finished mural.* Bottom: *One of the artist's studios.*
Inset: *A self-portrait — detail from the mural.* Opposite page: *The completed work.*

One who played a bigger part than most in this process was a young artist, from London, Robert Lenkiewicz, who turned thirty as he painted a spectacular mural on the McMullin's warehouse on the Parade.

Robert had moved down to Cornwall in 1968, with his wife Celia (Mouse) and daughter Alice. After a brief spell of teaching he came to Plymouth having been offered studio accommodation by local artist and businessman John Nash.

Soon after moving in, Robert, who had achieved notoriety in London for his support of 'dossers' and who continued that work in Plymouth, approached the City Council with a view to painting a large work on the wall next to his studio.

In a booklet published as 'Notes on the Barbican Mural', he publicly thanked the authorities and in particular, John Nash, the Barbican Association, Brolac (and their representatives for the supply of materials) and Harry Cooper *'without whose experience, common sense, and timing, nothing in this project would have been achieved'*. Completed in July 1972, after roughly ten months' work, the project is perhaps best described in extracts from the artist's own narrative.

'It is to be imagined that a large group of Elizabethan contemporaries numbering a little more than one hundred individuals are walking through an alley flanked by buildings …

'The theme of the mural concerns itself with metaphysical ideas current in England during the period 1580-1620.

'Although the presentation of the theme is subjective, the technique of painting is academic and traditional. The painting does not pretend to reflect any aspect of present day art theory.

'It is intended that the Barbican mural should convey some feeling of the demoniac brilliance of the Elizabethan age, a time of tremendous skills, flights of imaginations, and great brutalities, a time very much like our own.'

Referring to himself in the third person, Robert expressed the hope *'that the Painter will have further opportunity for several more mural projects in the City of Plymouth, and that they will be more adventurous in design'.*

Later, in a description of the figures portrayed he refers to a man pointing to contemporary coins and resting *'his right hand upon a skull, reminding one of the imminence of death'*. Oddly, he did not point out this particular portrait is of the impecunious artist himself.

Above: *The Royal Marine Band on the Parade, for Lord Mayor's Day outside the Old Custom House and Bill Hodges' Barbican Gallery.*
Inset: *Regatta programme.*

Further along the Parade, and across from the Custom House, was a building that had been twice saved from demolition, most recently after the Second World War — the old Custom House. In use in the Seventies as one of two bookmakers on the Barbican, this was run by a Plymouth-based turf accountant, Ron Hooper and his son Barry.

Curiously enough, the Parade is named the Parade because, before the Royal Marine Barracks were built in Durnford Street, the first contingent of Royal Marines in Plymouth were billeted in Southside Street and used this area as a parade ground. Thus, the Lord Mayor's Day picture opposite, is apposite.

Quay Road, incidentally, was built out from the Parade in the 1890s, when the Fish Market was constructed on reclaimed land by the Sutton Harbour Company.

In the Seventies the Sutton Harbour authorities were still allowing two-way traffic along its length, most of the year, but it was in their gift to close it as and when they wanted to, hence the regular appearance of the fairground

Top: *Quay Road.* Bottom: *Fairground and fishing boats.* Left: *The Big Wheel on the Quay.*

The Barbican with the former Crown & Anchor (Sir Francis Chichester) and the little-changed Dolphin Hotel.

Although the idea of lock gates across the harbour entrance had long been floated (Brunel had suggested it in 1845), Sutton Pool was still very much a tidal area in the Seventies. It was an issue of primary concern to fishermen and the occasional pleasure boat or private yachtsman.

Following the creation of seventy moorings off a single pontoon alongside Sutton Wharf in 1972, however, the number of harbour users increased significantly.

The moorings were snapped up within two weeks of becoming available, prompting the Sutton Harbour Company to double the number of moorings the following year.

Demand once again exceeded the supply and in 1974 the total number was increased to 200 and a year later there were still as many again on the waiting-list.

The popularity of this offer, combined with a sharp decline in the amount of mercantile vessels using the harbour, prompted a slow-but-sure series of changes around the waterfront.

The levels of warehousing required to service the port fell dramatically and owners were forced to think of alternative uses.

The Barbican Association converted a warehouse at the bottom of New Street into flats and, over at Vauxhall Quay, David King converted another and chose to occupy one of the flats himself. It was the beginning of a process that was to transform the Barbican.

General views of North Quay apart from Top right: Quay Road with fishing boats at very low tide.

The Barbican had not been noted for its social mix of housing for at least a hundred years or more and had done well to survive the various slum-clearance programmes that had been implemented from the 1890s onwards.

Indeed, it's remarkable how much had survived given that, in pursuing that particular agenda, the Local Authorities pulled down more Tudor and Jacobean buildings in the 10-15 years before the Second World War and again in the same time frame after the war, than enemy bombers had actually accounted for during the war.

The Lufftwaffe, though, had created some bomb-sites around the Barbican, but in comparative terms, relatively few. One of them, behind the Island House, and adjacent to the Green Lanterns restaurant, was redeveloped in 1971-2. The Barbican Association had owned one of the plots there and agreed to sell to the developer on the understanding that they had a say in the appearance of properties.

Above left and right: *Outside the Green Lanterns restaurant in New Street.*

The Barbican Association, an ad hoc organisation formed in 1957 to halt the seemingly wanton slum clearance process, were largely to thank for the area not being turned into a variation on post-war Devonport-by-the-Sea, with Looe Street and New Street containing the bulk of the property portfolio they acquired from the City.

In New Street they had possession of the complete stretch between numbers 34-40, all of which were late-sixteenth-, early-seventeenth-century properties and, in 1970, to commemorate the 350th anniversary of the sailing of the *Mayflower*, they commissioned the creation of the Elizabethan Gardens.

Having cleared all the poor-quality nineteenth-century tenement structures that had been erected behind the old houses, they invited the architect Alan Miller Williams to design gardens that would be in keeping with properties that backed on to them.

Borrowing bits of stonework from the City Engineers' Department, that is exactly what happened, and a wonderful tranquil area resulted.

Above left: *Inside the Elizabethan Gardens at the back of New Street.* Above right: *Looking out to sea past the Elizabethan House.*

The Barbican Association weren't the only landlords in New Street to have acquired buildings that were not, at that time, allowed to be used for domestic accommodation. Dennis and Mary Browning had numbers 43 and 44 New Street, on the site of the old Grey Friars Monastery. These they rented out to a variety of artists and crafts people. Potter Tony Evans occupied the ground floor of 43, along the side of Castle Dyke Lane, Robert Lenkiewicz had an attic room in 44 (mainly because it had a window overlooking the Jewish Cemetery), while the gifted landscape artist Chris Deakin had a room on the ground floor, as did the author of this tome, Chris Robinson, who at that time was working on a series of pen and ink sketches of the Barbican and old Plymouth generally.

The Fish Market was a popular subject, the sights, the sounds and the smells emanating from it conferring a distinctive ambience on the area.

All told there were over 30 little businesses up and down New Street and dozens more dotted around Southside Street, the Parade, Quay Road, and all the connecting opes and alleyways.

There was little in the way of bespoke tourist attractions, although the Elizabethan House was open weekdays 10am-6pm (but closed at lunchtime) and on Sundays for two hours in the afternoon from April to September.

Top left: *Inside the Fish Market*. Middle: *Fishing boat on White House Pier*. Left: *An early Chris Robinson print of the Barbican*. Above: *The China House*.

Drake's Island Ferry at the Mayflower Steps, with the Coal Wharf in the background.

Commercial Wharf and Elphinstone from Queen Anne Battery. Note the grassy slopes running down from the Citadel. Far right: Sailing into Sutton Harbour.

Beyond the East and West Piers there were a string of buildings and boathouses, the latter mainly under Commercial Road. Above the remnants of some biscuit factory buildings and Plymouth's original Victualling Yard, the military had laid out an assault course on the green slopes leading down from the Royal Citadel. The most conspicuous of the surviving structures in this stretch was the property serving as the Mayflower Sailing Club.

Standing alongside Phoenix Wharf, a regular departure point for pleasure boats, the Mayflower Sailing Club is said to be the last vestige of the old Emigration Depot that formerly filled most of the Elphinstone car park site, and which, for much of the nineteenth century, was the last piece of British soil that many an emigrant, typically bound for Australia, New Zealand or Canada, would have walked upon.

THE HOE

Whatever the attractions of the Barbican and Sutton Harbour, the real jewel-in-the-crown, as far as the City Fathers were concerned, was Plymouth Hoe.

Notwithstanding the Pilgrim Fathers' links with the old part of town, it was the Hoe that had the lion's share of the attention, from 1970 onwards. It was here that developers were encouraged to construct the two biggest hotels the City had ever seen, to cope with the anticipated influx of visitors from all over the world, but principally from America, whose citizens, they reasoned, would be keen to see precisely where their ancestors had last looked upon English soil.

Amazingly although, against the odds, much of the Barbican had survived, its 1620 street-plan little changed, while Plymouth Sound itself was barely altered from the time of Drake.

Happily, Mount Edgcumbe had retained its integrity as a country park, one of the finest in the country, and one of the few with a sea view, while on the other side of the Sound, Jennycliff, Staddon Heights and Bovisand, had largely escaped development.

Even Plymouth Hoe itself had obvious waterside areas where the rocks stretching up above the waterline were much as they had been for thousands of years. All those desirous of creating concrete walkways around the waterfront having been consistently turned down.

Meanwhile, the green open spaces below the Promenade constitute a public park with views that compete with those of any major city in the world.

Above: *Smeaton's Tower, white throughout the Seventies.* Opposite page: *Plymouth Hoe.*

The two new hotels were both opened in 1970, with crews working around the clock to try to meet the deadline.

Mike Luxton was one of those men, he was a crane driver for Kier Construction:

'I was two years or so on that job. Although the basic structure went up quite quickly — it went from first floor to top floor in about seven months — there was always plenty to do. Working every day, seven days a week at times, they even got a second crane driver in and it could be that work would finish at midnight some days as we were concreting through the night.'

To suggest he was part of the crew, however, is not a totally fair reflection on the job of a crane driver.

'It can be a fairly lonely existence though. I'd often get up in the crane and stay there all day. It wasn't a very big space, but you'd take your dinner up with you, and a radio … and an empty bottle.'

The obvious bonus, though, is that you get to see the world from a perspective few others are privy to, and Mike not only enjoyed it at the time, he also kept a photographic record of the job.

This page and opposite: *Working on the construction of the Holiday Inn, Plymouth*

It was, perhaps, no great surprise to find that the company behind this development was an American concern. The Holiday Inn chain had been started by a 39-year-old practicing Christian, Charles Kemmons Wilson. Wilson, who was from Memphis, had been on a family road trip to Washington and had been singularly unimpressed with the accommodation available along the way. And so he determined to build a better motel himself.

He commissioned architect Eddie Bluestein to draw up plans and the first motel was built on the aptly named Summer Avenue, the main route into Memphis from Nashville, in August 1952. The name, 'Holiday Inn' was suggested as a joke by Bluestein, a none-too-subtle reference to the Bing Crosby, Fred Astair movie of the same name.

It worked however, and the following year, with another practicing Christian, Wallace E Johnson, as his financial partner they built three more, each with a bible in every room.

Clean, family-friendly and mind-numbingly standard, there were over 100 Holiday Inns by 1959 and over 1,000 a decade later.

By 1972 they had become known as The World's Innkeeper.

Plymouth's Holiday Inn, opened in 1970.

Top: *The Holiday Inn sited just off the Hoe Park.* Above: *General view of the Hoe.*

Instantly advertising itself as the best hotel in Plymouth and the only four-star hotel in the City the Holiday Inn was certainly an instant novelty. The Penthouse Restaurant offered the sort of views only the dining facility on the top floor of the Civic Centre had previously made available, and that was primarily a daytime facility that soon afterwards was closed (in 1975) on public safety grounds.

There was also, on the top floor, the Poona Bar with its quirky collection of pith helmets, and downstairs, the Pier West Bar, soon to be restyled as the Pier West Wine Bar — all open to non-residents. Meanwhile, for those staying overnight, there was a choice of 225 big bedrooms, *'all with TV, radio, bath and shower as well as a sauna and indoor swimming pool'*.

By comparison, the Duke of Cornwall had around 70 bedrooms, the Continental 77, some *'with private bathrooms available'*, and the Berni Grand had 80.

Furthermore, the Holiday Inn's ample ballroom also made it a function favourite for fashion shows, annual dinner dances and a wide range of other major indoor events.

Looking back down Armada Way from the top of Smeaton's Tower.

Indoors

No. 83   THE JOURNAL OF THE TRUST HOUSES GROUP   SUMMER 1970

The Mayflower Post House, opened in May 1970. Inset left: The Mayflower Bar.

The big question in those early days was, how would the other hotels compete? Particularly the other new inn with arguably even better views at the end of the Hoe Promenade.

As it transpired it seems as though the two were never really in direct competition, while the Holiday Inn set its sights on high standards, the Mayflower Post House was looking to provide 'high standards of comfort at low rates'.

Adjudged 'Britain's best new hotel' by the British Tourist Authority when it opened in May 1970, the hotel had 102 bedrooms and two penthouse suites, each with 'private bathroom, telephone, radio and television, plus free tea and coffee making facilities.' Here the emphasis was on 'good planning and design' and 'minimising room service and passing on the savings'.

Like the Holiday Inn it had it own 'first-class Restaurant, with its own bar' and a 'Buttery serving inexpensive light meals and grills whenever you want them — from early morning to late evening'.

The Buttery was quintessentially Seventies with its 'interesting "stalactite ceiling lights and a gay decorative theme of signal flags'.

Jeanette Hopkins was one of the 30 or so girls hired to work there:

'There was an advertisement for Hotel Hostesses in the Herald about six months before it opened and, like Air Hostesses, they had to be trained in all aspects of hotel work table-waiting, bar-work, reception etc.

'The training took place at the Continental Hotel, while the Mayflower was being built.'

The Continental was then, like the Mayflower Post House, a Trust House Forte hotel. Curiously enough, the Trust House Forte brand was a 1970 amalgam that followed on from the merger that year of the Trust Houses Group and Forte Holdings.

Forte Holdings was a UK company that had been founded by the British/Italian caterer-cum-hotelier Charles Forte. Forte had set up his first 'Milk Bar', in 1926, in Regent Street, London while still in his twenties. After the war his enterprise continued to expand and in 1960 he opened Britain's first full motorway service station for cars, at Newport Pagnell.

By 1970, the Trust House empire included almost 200 hotels, motels and inns and it would have been a mighty relief to all concerned that the Mayflower was open and ready for business on 1 May, the day before Plymouth's *Mayflower* celebrations were scheduled to start.

Top : *View from the outdoor pool.* Right: *The Buttery Bar.*

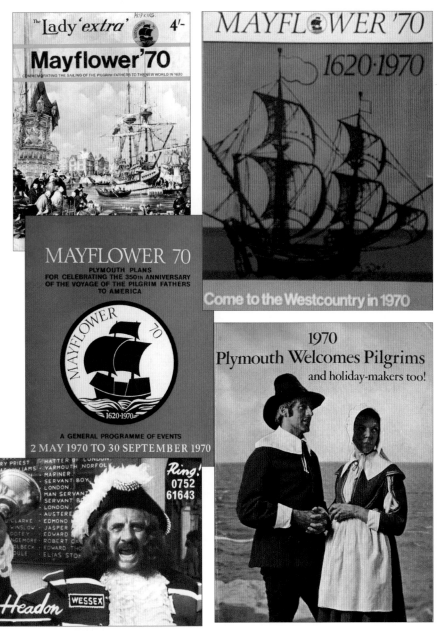

This page: *Various brochures, guides and programmes for Mayflower '70.*
Above left: *Plymouth Town Crier, Ken Headon.*

'It was a chaotic year,' recalled Jeanette, 'the hotel was heaving with Americans, but I don't think all the girls had enough training'.

At the official opening of the Mayflower Post House, on Wednesday 13 May 1970, the Lord Mayor of Plymouth said: 'As far as Plymouth is concerned this is a great new day. The City has long been planning for a new hotel worthy of this site. We think it is the finest in Britain.'

There could be little doubt that Local Authorities had done their best to milk the Mayflower Celebrations for all they could.

Two prime sites had been allocated for the construction of the two biggest hotels the City had ever seen and a full programme of events had been booked across the summer to entertain the thousands of anticipated visitors.

Graham Mayhew, graphic designer to the Royal Shakespeare Company, was commissioned to produce a *'Come to the Westcountry in 1970'* poster that was produced in association with BOAC (British Overseas Airways Corporation — it became British Airways in 1974), and distributed around the world.

'Get details from your travel agent', the poster enthused. Meanwhile, Sir Ronald Brockman, Chairman of the Mayflower '70 Committee, wrote in volume six of the somewhat flimsy and overpriced (2/6d) 'Plymouth '70' 12-page magazine: 'We are confident that this celebration, between May 2 and September 30, will be worthy of the event it commemorates. Our greatest reward will be to see people enjoying themselves in our country at this time.'

There were programmes, posters, brochures, trails, seals, stamps, models and even a Pilgrim's Passport that admitted the bearer to *'fourteen places of interest in Plymouth and District'* — a snip at £1.10s.0d (£1.50).

The Junior Chamber produced a set of 10 sticky seals that you could buy in a cardboard wallet for a shilling (5p) while the GPO issued a special commemorative *Mayflower* stamp on 1 April 1970.

The *Mayflower* Anniversary was one of a set of five anniversaries being recognised with those particular issues, the Declaration of Arbroath, the birth of Florence Nightingale, the International Cooperative Alliance and the founding of the Astronomical Society being the others.

Of the five, the *Mayflower* stamp would appear to have had the greatest potential for exploitation as not only was there a special Plymouth postmark available on 1 April, but also on the 2 May, 4 June, 6 September ... Dartmouth got in on the act too, with a 2 September mark, whereas Southampton exploited their 15 August link with 1620.

There were also various static models around, illustrating scenes of Plymouth from 1620, and a grand *'Animated Model Town'* with fully animated and illuminated scenes of the period when the Pilgrim Fathers were at Plymouth'.

Situated on the ground floor of the Mayflower Offices, by Derry's Clock, the model could be viewed daily from 2 May, 10am to 8pm, and on Sunday 10.30am to 5.30pm: adults 2/6d, children 1/6d.

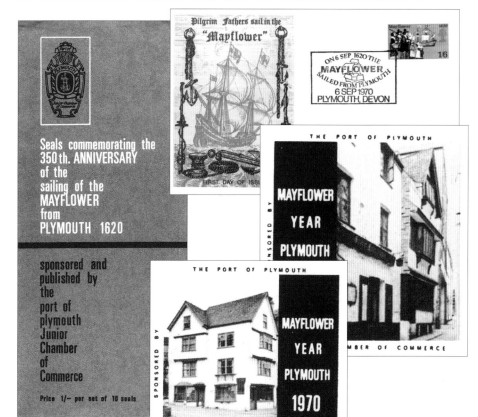

This page: A selection of Mayflower '70 stamps, seals and first day covers

Derry's Cross windmill installation — part of the Mayflower '70 Dutch Fortnight celebrations.

The programme of events began on that first Saturday in May.

After the grand opening bash on the Hoe, Senator Leverett Saltanstall, a descendant of a Pilgrim Father and representing the Governor of Massachusetts, declared open 'Massachusetts Week', which was followed by a Dutch Fortnight, then a 'Drake Week', and an 'Army Week'…

And so it went on through the summer of 1970. There was a 'Come to the United States' Fortnight, a 'Royal Air Force Week', a 'Sea-Angling Week', a 'Royal Navy Week', a cringingly titled 'Keenage Week' — *'a special exhibition for young people in the exhibition hall'*, as well as a 'Young Executives' Week' — a nod to the fact that the National Conference of the British Chamber of Commerce (Junior) was being staged in the City that September. And last, but by no means least, as it related more directly to what the whole bean feast was supposed to be about in the first place a 'Pilgrims' Week'. There were, spread across the summer, a number of pageants, exhibitions and shows that had a degree of relevance like the Carmenians' presenting a world premier of Connor and Cutter's *Mayflower* — a musical that had been gathering dust since it was written 13 years earlier to commemorate the sailing of the *Mayflower* replica.

Essentially, however, the programme was fleshed out with events that would have been happening anyway and had nothing to do with the events of 1620, like: horse racing at Haldon and Newton Abbot; the Courage Men's Darts League Championships, Exeter Air Show and Harry Corbett with Sooty at the Hoe Theatre.

Top left: *A Mayflower event inside the Citadel.* Bottom left: *Pilgrim's Week.* Above: *22-year-old Sandra Ann Ritchie — Miss Mayflower '70.*

Of the 400 or so, so-called Mayflower '70 events, the vast majority were entirely irrelevant and in the absence of an easy means of advising City Entertainments Officer, Frank Bottom, and the organisers of the programme, what they thought of their trip to Plymouth that summer, one can but wonder as to the long-term impact of the celebrations. Although, as Jeanette Hopkins at the Mayflower Hotel recalls, one of her female co-hostesses *'hitched up with an Amercian guest and went over to the States'*, so the hoped for benefits to Anglo-American relations worked in one corner at least.

Throughout the Seventies the Hoe, as ever, hosted the majority of the City's biggest and most popular events. Most of these were free affairs and at times the crowds could be very large indeed.

Lord Mayor's Day was a perennial favourite and business organisations, social groups, and societies regularly invested hours of their time in producing and manning an impressive array of floats — some more overtly commercial than others.

Meanwhile, another regular visitor to the Hoe was the Radio 1 Roadshow. Brainchild of Radio 1 producer Johnny Beerling, the first ever of these touring extravaganzas was staged in Newquay in 1973 and Plymouth quickly established itself as a favourite on the annual itinerary as Tony Miles 'Smiley Miley' moved the colourful caravan around the country.

Vintage car shows, bus rallies, and air displays also attracted big crowds to the Hoe ... and its attendant cafés.

Left: *Lord Mayor's Day 1971*. Top left: *Welcome to Plymouth floral display*.
Top right: *The Radio 1 Roadshow with Dave Lee Travis*. Bottom right: *The hatchback Vauxhall Chevette is shown off at Lord Mayor's Day*.

Clockwise from left: *A selection of Hoe cafés — West Hoe Pier Café, the Hoe Café and the Mallard Café under Smeaton's Tower and the liner lookout.*

There was a reasonable choice of cafés for the time: the Lyons Maid-run Hoe Café, a curious post-war hangar creation that stood in behind the statue of Drake, on the site of the more substantial pre-war café; the still quite new, Mallard below Smeaton's Tower and another at West Hoe, next to the Royal Western Yacht Club. There were also a number of different tea and pasty outlets around Tinside Pool.

On a sunny summer's day this was a huge draw and attracted locals and visitors alike. Although there were other facilities in the city, there was, potentially, the only straight 50-yard swim from side to side available here, although seldom was it quiet enough to make the distance without bumping into someone.

For those perhaps not so keen to splash about and soak up the sun, the Hoe still had plenty else to offer the visitor, including: the aquarium housed in the Marine Biological Association in front of the Royal Citadel; the Hoe Theatre, which generally had a special summer show offering fun for all the family, and Smeaton Tower (as it was referred to).

This was open to the public daily, from 10.30 am until one hour before sunset, from the end of April until the beginning of October. The cost of admission was 7p, although for parties of 20 or more there was a special concessionary price of 5p. Advance booking was through the City Engineer's Office in the Civic Centre.

Tinside Pool particularly popular in the long, hot summer of 1976.

West Hoe, with the Royal Western Yacht Club and the tennis courts across the road.

Other recreational opportunities in and around the Hoe included an 18-hole putting green, just down from the Hoe Theatre; a crazy golf putting course at West Hoe, where there were also some fine public tennis courts. In addition there was an annual round of *'Holiday Bowls Competitions'* every Thursday during the *'High Season'*.

For those who didn't particularly want to do anything much at all, except enjoy the sun and stunning views, there were deck chairs for hire or, if you really wanted to push the boat out, beach huts for hire. With lockers, tables and chairs, the huts were available for day use only. There were some on the foreshore, at Tinside and Pebbleside, with others sited slightly further afield at Devil's Point.

The rules were quite strict, however: applications had to be made to the Tourist Information Centre in the Civic Centre, but no applications were considered until the first day of January in the year the hut was required. Day bookings could only be made if there was a hut available and couldn't be made in advance. Needless to say, most were snapped up by locals.

Left: *Crazy golf at West Hoe.* Right: *Soaking up the sun at Tinside.*

For those feeling truly adventurous, though, there was always Drake's Island.

Host to one of the festival weeks during Mayflower '70, Drake's Island offered its own unique views of the City and the Sound, but more than that it provided *'a variety of exciting courses for residential and non-residential individuals and groups between 8-60 years.*

'General courses,' ran the City's tourist guide of 1977, *'include sailing, canoeing, orienteering and marine biology.*

'Further courses can be taken to National Qualification in sailing and canoeing.'

The brochure continued: *'Also available are twin venue weeks, combining a course on Drake's Island and cruising the Scilly Isles or the Channel/France.*

'Evening leisure time activities for residents involve, barbeques, film shows, discos and shore visits.

'The ferry service provides frequent visitor access to Drake's Island and includes an interesting guided tour.' In fairness the weather meant that sometimes the island wasn't accessible, but it was beautiful when it was, although the rats in the unlit gun emplacements could be scary!

Above: *Drake's Island*. Opposite page, top: *Stanley Goodman looks out over the island*. Middle: *View the city*. Bottom: *Drake's Island Café and the view from the Island*.

Plymouth Hoe and Millbay Docks c.1979.

MILLBAY AND STONEHOUSE

brittany ferries

Plymouth's waterfront underwent a fairly major revamp during the Seventies, much of it to do with a move away from industry and merchant trading, towards tourism and leisure.

If it was apparent in Sutton Harbour and around the entrance to Stonehouse Creek it was even more obvious in Millbay Docks.

Some of it was occasioned by the removal of rail connections, some of it by Britain's ever-diminishing role as a manufacturing base.

However, in none of these locations did it mark the end of their viability. Just as Sutton Harbour was being re-invented as a niche shopping, dining and drinking area, with marinas alongside, so Millbay became an international ferry port.

It was at precisely seven o'clock in the morning on 3 January 1973 that the French ferry ship *Kerisnel* dropped her stern door in Millbay and opened Plymouth's door to the EEC. The first vehicle driven ashore, having made the crossing from Roscoff, brought a load of cauliflowers from Brittany.

Millbay Docks had undergone quite an upheaval in order to accommodate the new Brittany Ferry traffic and the *Kerisnel* was the company's first vessel.

A modest craft tipping the scales at 3,395 tonnes, the Spanish-built ship (originally destined to be called MV *Lilac*), had just twelve cabins. Less than a year old when she arrived, the *Kerisnel* was in the service of Brittany Ferries little more than twelve months, as she was sold (and renamed MV *La Durance*) when the company took delivery of their own, specially commissioned new vessel *Pen-ar-Bed*, in 1974.

Four years later traffic into and out of Millbay increased further as the ferry company introduced an additional new route, to Santander.

Top: Kerisnel *arrives in Plymouth*. Bottom *The Russian ferry MS* Odessa

Apart from these exciting new links with France and Spain, a number of vessels visited the port with much greater distances in mind.

On a number of occasions across the decade the docks were the rallying point for boats taking part in various major sailing competitions, most notably the Observer Transatlantic Single-Handed Yacht Race, and the Tall Ships Race.

Each time hundreds of spectators would turn out to see the skippers preparing their craft, each one remarkable in its own way, whether a single-hulled ship, catamaran, trimaran or something altogether more impressive. One of the most spectacular visitors had to be the splendid three-masted Norwegian training ship, the *Christian Radich*.

Requiring a crew of 18 and capable of accommodating 88 passengers, she was here for the Tall Ships race in 1970 and again 1976. Doubtless she pulled in the biggest crowds on her second visit as by then the *Christian Radich* had become a true star in her own right, having appeared as herself, as one of James Onedin's vessels, in the classic TV series, the Onedin Line – which the BBC ran from 1971 through to 1980.

The Observer Single-Handed race, starting out from here in 1972 and 1976, was dominated by the French, most notably Eric Tabarly in his celebrated trimaran, *Pen Duick IV* which won on both occasions. Brian Cooke, in *British Steel*, was the leading Brit in 1972 – he came fourth. Sir Francis Chichester, then aged 70, took part in the race but was forced to withdraw. Sadly the intrepid sailor — and aviator — died later that year.

Top: *Boats prepare for the Single-Handed Transatllantic Race.*
Bottom: *Preparing for the tall ships.*

Admiral's Cup Winner, Prime Minister, Ted Heath, at the end of the race in Millbay, 1971, with the Herald's Ken Fenn, far right.

Entrants making ready for the Tall Ships Race.

Looking at Union Street from the air at the end of the Seventies gives us the perfect vantage point to see just how far the plans towards dualling the carriageway from Stonehouse bridge had been implemented. East of Western Approach, in the town end of the street, a dual carriageway was already in place, and west of the old border between Plymouth and Stonehouse (along the line of Manor Street and Phoenix Street) it was increasingly clear that the piecemeal removal of buildings along the way was making the ultimate success of the plan more and more likely, as all of the post-war premises being erected were springing up some distance behind the original street line.

It's also evident to what extent another element of the 1943 Plan was still being adhered to, and that was the proposal to concentrate domestic housing to the north of Union Street and keep commercial and industrial operations to the south of the street.

As mentioned earlier, however, the listing of the Palace Theatre thwarted parts of that policy and consequently the stretch between the Palace and the Odeon was largely left as it was after the war, apart from the obvious infilling of one or two bomb sites.

Incidentally, the Odeon, which had been known as the Gaumont prior to the demolition of the earlier Odeon in New George Street (originally known as the Regent), only just managed to see out the decade as a cinema. It had already been reconfigured in the Sixties by the Rank Organisation to form a smaller cinema with ballroom, but following on from both the ABC and the Drake going down the multi-screen path, falling numbers made it increasingly unviable.

Opposite page: *Union Street from the air, 1979.* This page, top right: *Union Street from Flora Street.* Bottom right: *West Hoe from the air.* Bottom left: *Union Street going to seed.*

This page: *The old Plymouth Brewery and Prince George pub disappear from the scene.*

As if to emphasise the ever-changing post-war appearance of the City, the changes didn't end with Union Street. Heading towards Stonehouse bridge, other local landmarks that disappeared around this time were the early nineteenth-century Prince George Hotel, the slightly later, neighbouring Plymouth Brewery complex and what had been Devonport's Electricity station, albeit on the Stonehouse side of the creek.

Before long a series of giant sheds had spread across the sites — part of the expanding empire of Princess Yachts, a company that had grown spectacularly since its beginnings in Newport Street in 1965. Meanwhile, at the far end of Durnford Street out at Western Kings and Devil's Point, Plymothians were still getting used to the idea that they could walk or drive out to the end of the Stonehouse Peninsula and enjoy a walk or a picnic on a site that had been considered crucial to the defence of the port and that the Government had only, comparatively recently, released.

At the same time on the other side of Firestone Bay, the Edgcumbe's old winter villa, which since 1932 had been in the hands of the Sisters of Nazareth, was pulled down and a new Nazareth House was erected.

Devil's Point, Firestone Bay and Nazareth House.

This page: *Ocean Court Marina appears on the site of the former Ocean Quay Terminal (inset).*
Opposite page: *Ocean Court across from the Royal William Victualling Yard.*

Further up the coastline, on the northern bank of the entrance to Stonehouse Creek, at the far end of Richmond Walk, the closure, in 1970, of Ocean Quay railway terminal, meant that there was potential for a major development here, just as there was at Millbay. In the event, however, the Millbay site was to remain largely in limbo throughout the Seventies. The transformation of Ocean Quay, on the other hand, began very soon after the land became available.

Offering excellent views across the Tamar Estuary, the site was soon lined with the City's first residential Marina. Constructed in a style reminiscent of the luxury liners of the day, the new 82-flat, 200-berth, development was christened Ocean Court Marina in reference to the fact that, like Millbay, this railway terminal had once serviced the transatlantic liner trade.

Back in the day, the trains from Ocean Quay competed with those from Millbay in the quest to whisk their passengers up to London as quickly as possible.

Before the age of commercial flights, the reality was that either route was quicker for those making the transatlantic crossing, as the alternative was to stay on the ship until it reached Southampton.

However, there was a nasty accident in the summer of 1906 when a London and South Western train out of Ocean Quay was derailed on account of going too fast through Salisbury. Essentially the driver attempted to take a 30mph curve at 70 mph: 24 passengers were killed and the 'racing' was stopped.

Not long afterwards Ocean Quay's days as a passenger terminal were terminated, although the station continued to provide a goods service for another 60 years.

On the opposite side of the entrance to Stonehouse Creek, incidentally, the impressive early-nineteenth-century Royal William Victualling Yard was heading towards its 150th anniversary as a Royal Naval supply base, however its architectural treasures were something of a mystery to most Plymothians.

Mount Wise, surmounted by Onslow House with part of South Yard in the distance.

DEVONPORT

The opening up of Richmond Walk in the wake of the Ocean Court development was to be followed by other moves that would give public access to hitherto 'no go' areas.

Mount Wise had been a popular outdoor swimming venue since the new pool, at what had been known as Bullock's Dock, was first opened back in 1923. Since then, it seems, there had hardly been a school in Plymouth that had not, at some point, held its annual swimming events here, most accessing the area via James Street and Mutton Cove.

Mount Wise itself was dominated by Admiralty House, Government House and Seymour House, all owned by the MOD. During the Second World War a veritable warren of tunnels and chambers had been dug out under the green, sea-facing slopes and here the nerve centre of the Western Command (MHQ Maritme Headquarters) was established, virtually bomb-proof and complete with its own generators.

Meanwhile, on the site of the former Mount Wise Redoubt, the naval residences known as Onlsow House, looked out over the Hamoaze.

Above: *Mount Wise swimming pool, scene of so many school swimming galas, with the Royal William Yard in the distance.*
Inset: *Jane Maddox, picks up a swimming trophy for Plymouth High School for Girls at Mount Wise, 1974.*

By 1970, however, Mount Wise was no longer operating as a nerve centre, its subterranean corridors had long been silent and after 25 years of comparative peace, the level of activity in the area generally, had fallen away.

In the ten-year period 1961-1971, employment in the shipbuilding sector declined from 56% to 43% of manufacturing in the Plymouth travel-to-work area. The last warship to have been constructed in the Dockyard, HMS *Sylla*, had slipped into the Hamoaze in 1968 and by the end of the Seventies, the two big, pre-war cantilever cranes either side of slip No.3 had been cut down. Furthermore the outlook for the other cranes wasn't promising.

The facility was far from being a spent force however, and even before the Dockyard had been re-designated as Devonport Naval Base in 1970, the first of a series of major projects were announced. First up was the news, broken by the then Navy Minister and MP for Devonport, Dr David Owen, in October 1969, that a new operational base was to be established, in North Yard, in support of nuclear-powered submarines.

Dock walls were removed, new ones built and whole areas refashioned to accommodate the new proposals. North Lock became two separate locks and early in 1972 the conventional submarine *Otus* became the first to float in to the newly formed No.11 Dock, while the first nuclear vessel, *Valiant*, entered No.12 Dock in December of that year.

The work by no means ended there though: Stage 2 involving the actual construction of the Complex, began in 1975.

A giant, 80-ton cantilever crane, specifically designed to lift nuclear core packages weighing up to 72 tonnes each, became a new feature on the landscape, alongside a new, eight-storey management office at one end and a nine-storey submarine support facility in the middle (that had five storeys above and four below).

In the event, it wasn't until 1980 that the Submarine Refit Complex was officially opened, by Prince Charles, on Friday 23 May.

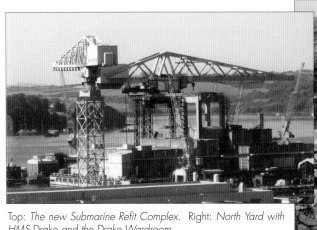

Top: *The new Submarine Refit Complex.* Right: *North Yard with* HMS Drake *and the Drake Wardroom.*

One of the knock-on effects of the decision to site the Submarine Refit Complex in North Yard was the need to have better shore-side support for the growing number of ships and submarines using Devonport.

HMS *Forth* had initially been charged with that role following the arrival of the submarines in 1972, and, after a brief refit, was recommissioned for the job as HMS *Defiance*. But before long demand had outstripped *Defiance*'s capabilities and the decision was taken to create a new Fleet Maintenance Base on shore and close to the Submarine Refit Complex.

The fully equipped facility meant that all essential repairs and renewals could be carried out as close as was physically possible to the craft being refitted.

Offices, stores and workshops were built so that electronic equipment could be tried and treated, periscopes could be raised and calibrated, and stores could be replaced and replenished.

A new jetty, to provide new berths, was constructed on the edge of Weston Mill Lake, and was linked to the mainland via a short bridge to the foreshore of the Royal Naval Barracks — HMS *Drake*.

As another vote of confidence in Devonport, the new facility was officially opened on 21 April 1978 by the Prime Minister, James Callaghan.

It was an impressive addition to the Naval Base's offer and it augmented another resource that had been opened almost a year earlier, further down the river.

It had been back in January 1970 that David Owen, by then wearing his Parliamentary Under Secretary of State for Defence (Navy) hat, had announced plans to create an indoor Frigate Complex in the Keyham Yard.

Top: *Prime Minister James Callaghan opens the new Fleet Maintenance Base in April 1978.* Above: Ark Royal Christmas leave, 1971.
Right: *View from the crane at Submarine Refit Base.*

The Frigate Complex transformed the Naval Base's ability to work on ships whatever the weather. Furthermore, the facilities for connecting ships docked in the Complex to electricity supplies, air conditioning and sewage disposal, meant that it was possible for the ship's company to live, eat and sleep on board ship throughout the refitting process.

The massive doors of the £18 million Complex were constructed to rise to a height of 160ft and were fabricated in four sections, each capable of independent action, so that the top part could be lowered to allow for natural ventilation. The first official flooding of the new complex took place during the long hot, and ultimately, very dry summer of 1976, on 2 June. However, it wasn't until the following year that the first ship, the Leander class frigate HMS *Galatea*, entered the facility. Very much a trial move, in March, it wasn't until May that the Complex was properly put into working use, with the admission of the Devonport-built HMS *Cleopatra*.

Galatea, incidentally, was back on hand to give a demonstration docking later that summer, on 23 September, when Dr David Owen returned to his Devonport constituency on official business, to formally declare the striking new Complex open.

As she entered No.6 Dock the Royal Marine Band did their best to fill the indoor facility with music.

Meanwhile other, smaller-scale Seventies' developments in the Yard included a new £285,000 restaurant (March 1971); a new Yard Services Workshop in North Yard (April 1972); a 169-metre long Pipe Shop (March 1975), and a purpose-built Medical Centre, close to St Levan Gate (November 1979).

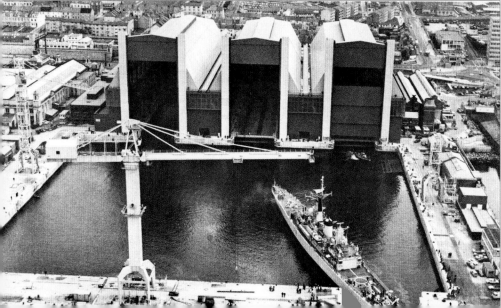

Top left:: *David Owen MP opens the impressive new Frigate Complex, in September 1976.* Left: HMS Galatea *entering the main basin in 1977.* Above: *General view of the new facility.*

New buildings dominate this view from Devonport Park of the Victorian Steamyard.

Top: *In 1978 the* Eagle *returned and the* Ark Royal *(pictured) departed.*
Bottom: *May 1976, the Raglan Estate is opened.*

Another Seventies initiative of some significance was the decision to accept female apprentices. In 1970 advertisements were sent out and some 60 enquiries were received: as it transpired, however, only nine girls ended up completing application forms of whom only seven sat the entrance examination.

Only one of the girls failed to pass, but four of the six successful candidates changed their minds about becoming Dockyardies, which left two, one of whom failed the interview stage.

Happily the other girl passed the interview and was offered a place, subject to her attaining certain grades in her GCE 'O' Levels. Unfortunately she didn't attain those grades and so there were no girls taken on that year.

On a brighter note, the following year 21 girls sat the exams, 14 passed and eight of them ended up becoming apprentices, alongside that year's entry of 230 boys.

All of this extra construction work and the extension of job opportunities for women didn't mean that all was well in the workplace, however. On a couple of occasions in the Seventies work was brought to a halt over disputes concerning terms and conditions.

In 1972 there were strikes over pay that culminated in a week's action that September. At the other end of the decade, Civil Servants in the Naval Base staged a walk-out, affecting the work being done on various refit programmes and once again, in June 1979, work was almost brought to a standstill.

Such unrest wasn't confined to Devonport. Nationally it was a time of great industrial unrest. The miner's strike in 1972 had prompted a power crisis and precipitated the necessity of a three-day working week. Growing dissatisfaction also ousted the Conservative Government under Edward Heath, but the situation didn't ease and inflation rose to a record 25%.

The inflation rate wasn't the only element contributing to domestic difficulties in the Seventies. The situation in Northern Ireland was also causing problems on the mainland and following a succession of bomb attacks in England and Northern Ireland itself, servicemen were banned from wearing uniform outside of military or naval bases. A generation of Britons had grown up knowing only peace in Europe and now internal troubles were causing grief, as race riots, too, flared up in London, Liverpool, Birmingham and other major cities around the country ... but not in Plymouth.

Top: *Torpoint Ferry.* Above: *On board*
Middle: *Pottery Quay flats looking across to Harvey's coal yard.*
Far left and left: *Two views of the Tamar Canal one looking inland to the Tamar Brewery, the other looking out towards the Hamoaze.*

The Tamar Road Bridge.

AROUND THE CITY

As the Seventies dawned, the Saltash Ferry was fast becoming a distant memory as the Tamar Road bridge was entering it's tenth year of operation.

The cost of crossing, at the time of the tenth anniversary of it's opening by the Queen Elizabeth, the Queen Mother, in 1962, was 10p per car, one new penny per bicycle and 2.5p per motorcycle.

You could halve those rates if you were prepared to buy a book of 20 tickets and the same deal applied to coaches and heavy goods vehicles for whom the basic rate was 45p a crossing. The rates were identical for the Torpoint ferry and tickets were interchangeable.

Curiously enough, no rate was given in the guide books for cars towing caravans, a reflection perhaps on the comparative rarity of the combination at the time.

By the end of the Sixties the number of new caravans that were registered in one year was 53,000, almost three times what it had been a decade earlier. In the Seventies that number continued its upward spiral, with one company alone (Caravans International) producing 35,000 touring vans in one calendar year.

But, as the decade progressed, the City, still advertising itself as the Centre of 100 Tours, didn't include touring vans in its guide book tariffs.

It's interesting to note though that by 1976 the cost of crossing had increased by 50% for car drivers (to 15p), 55% for coaches and heavy goods and 60% for motorbikes, but still stayed at a penny for pushbikes.

The last Torpoint ferry, incidentally, ran each night at 1.15am.

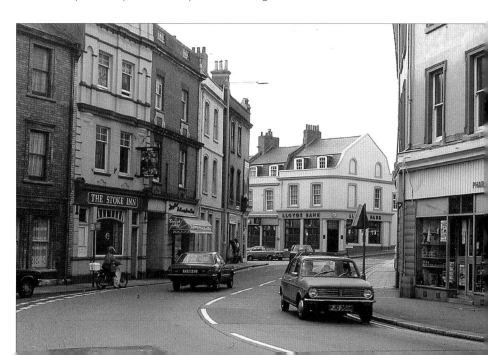

Two views of Stoke Village.

Main image: *Bernard Mill's June 1970 shot looking towards Milehouse Junction.*
Inset top: *The Britannia and the Embassy Club.* Left: *Milehouse depot.*

Left: *The Britannia.*
Above: *The Police Box in Outland Road.*
Below: *Outland Road, June 1970.*

Buses were still a primary means of transportation for vast numbers of local commuters. Slowly but surely the old open-backed step-on step-off Metro Cammell Leylands were being phased out and being replaced by a new fleet of Leyland Atlanteans.

These rear-engine, front-entrance vehicles had first appeared on the streets of Plymouth in 1960 and by the end of that decade Plymouth City Transport had begun the process of converting them to one-man operated affairs.

In 1970 the company took delivery of nineteen dual Atlanteans which undoubtedly made life easier as passengers paid on the way in but could exit without getting in the way of those trying to pay. Interestingly enough, PCT were the first operators in the South West to introduce the one-man bus idea and to further simplify things they brought in fares that were in multiples of thruppence.

In December 1975, and well post-decimalisation, fare stages of .85 miles were brought in to make life easier still. That same year single-decker buses reappeared on Plymouth streets as a consignment of Leyland Nationals were added to the PCT fleet. Smoking was banned on these vehicles.

Principal routes around the City passed through a number of places that still had an independent air about them.

St Budeaux Square was lined with shops that catered for most everyday needs.

The only pub in any direction, for some distance, the Trelawney, sat at the hub of the commercial community, although clearly the times were changing and an Off Licence occupied the site that had long ago been the entrance to the stabling facilities for the village inn.

Horses, which had not been an unknown sight on the city's streets as late as the 1950s, were seldom seen in the Seventies as the relentless rise of the motor car occasioned road-widening programmes in many locations.

Wolseley Road, running from Milehouse to St Budeaux Square lost two Southern Railway bridges in the early Seventies as part of a £28,000 road improvement and embankment removal project that was completed in August 1972.

Earlier that same year, in March, a whole row of houses was demolished over a single weekend in Peverell, as Hermon Terrace was wiped away to improve the access from Milehouse to Manadon.

Top: *21 September 1971, St Budeaux Square.* Middle: *Lord Mayor Arthur Floyd re-opens the Co-op Tamar House store at St Budeaux 1977.* Bottom: *Bridge clearance, Weston Mill, 1971.* Right: *Hermon Terrace Peverell early 1972.*

Bottom: *Hermon Terrace demolished over one weekend in 1972.* Top: *West Park in the Seventies.* Right: *Ham and Burrington c.1973.*

Beyond Manadon, the northern route out of Plymouth had already seen great changes in the late-Sixties — Crownhill village had been completely bypassed.

In 1968 the old Plumer Barracks site had been cut through and a sweeping new dual-carriageway up Manadon Hill had been laid out. A second phase of development saw the erection of Plymouth's new Divisional Police Headquarters in Crownhill, in 1976, following the departure of the last infantry battalion to have been based in Plymouth. The garrison church of St Alban's, Plumer Barracks, was shut.

Meanwhile, the apparently well-founded fears surrounding the bypassing of the village were at last being allayed as shopkeepers in Crownhill were starting to notice signs that the worst of the depression might be over.

'The prosperous shopping centre patronized daily by hundreds of people reverted virtually overnight to what it was in the distant past – a quiet peaceful village,' noted one local trader. But, at long last, things were looking up. In June 1971 Councillor Ralph Morrell opened John Pascoe's bright new Post Office in the village.

Top left: *Golden Hind at Manadon, February 1974.* Left: *Crownhill Village.*
Inset: *Ralph Morrell opens John Pascoe's Post Office 1971.*
Above: *Site cleared for Crownhill Police Station, 1971.*

Above: *Roy Perring's aerial shot of Crownhill c.1979.*
Inset: *A police crime recreation shot from 1976, taken at the former HQ in Greenbank.*

Another area with an almost village-like presence was Mutley Plain. The hub of Plymouth's retail offer for the first ten years or so after the Blitz, Mutley Plain, at the start of the Seventies, was still very well provided for, with its own fishmonger, butchers, bakers, grocers, chemists, furniture store, cinema, supermarket, newsagents, record shop, electrical goods stores, Post Office and pubs — three of them: the Hyde Park, Fortescue and Nottingham.

It also had two major churches, Mutley Baptist and Mutley Methodist. The former celebrated its centenary in 1969 while the latter was denied the opportunity to do the same just a few years later.

Completed and consecrated in 1881, Mutley Methodist, well-remembered for the full-size nativity scene that decorated its front entrance at Christmas time, was closed in 1977 and pulled down in 1979, two years short of its big anniversary.

At the southern end of the thoroughfare, in Houndiscombe Road, directly opposite Lipton's supermarket, which was located in one of Mutley's few post-war buildings, was another post-war structure, the former Welfare State related building just along from Mutley Baptist. This, in the Seventies, was the Driving Test Centre, where many a Plymothian headed with heavy heart, hoping that, for the duration of the test at least, they wouldn't put a foot wrong!

Top left: *Mutley Plain, 1971*. Left: *Mutley Plain in 1979 without Mutley Methodist Church*. Above: *An early Seventies view, still with the church, from the other end.*

Above: *Another Roy Perring aerial from 1979 looking over Deer Park* Left: *Driving Test Centre, Houndiscombe Road.*

Left: *Looking towards Cattedown Road bridge between Julian Street, left and Mainstone Avenue, right in 1973.* Above: *Prince Rock and the Western National Bus Station c.1979.*

While Mutley Plain was the main arterial route out of the City Centre heading north, for all eastern bound traffic it was Embankment Road. Here again there was a wide variety of retail outlets, mainly, it must be said, on one side, which wasn't, for the most part, the sunny side of the street.

The volume of traffic travelling along it had been growing substantially over the years and the potential for congestion, as well as for accidents, was growing all the time.

While the widening of Embankment Road itself was seriously problematic, improvements to the Embankment, along the edge of the Laira were less complicated. There were a few casualties resulting from the work however, among them the demolition, in 1971, of the ancient Crabtree Inn, and the loss of Laira Wharf, or the 'Tide' as it was known locally — the little tidal harbour that was to be found on the landward side of the railway tracks. Blagdon's Boatyard was to be found here, as was part of the route of Thomas Tyrwhitt's pre-steam, horse-drawn railway.

By 1973 the job had been completed and the dual-carriageway leading to Marsh Mills was opened. Meanwhile, as the rail links to Sutton Harbour and Cattedown became redundant, so vast tracts of land lay idle, with who knew what plans for their future.

A selection of Bernard Mills' images. Above One of the last Plymouth City Transport's Leyland PD2s makes one final circuit, seen here on the recently redundant crossing at Cattedown in 1974. Top right: The Warship Class 'Zenith' coming off Laira Shed, September 1970. Middle: Laira Wharf. Right: The new dual carriageway in use, October 1973.

Above: *October 1970, the Branch Line Society Area Rail Tour makes a late crossing of the Plym.*
Left: *5 February 1971, Plymouth Power Station.*

There was a similar story on the other side of the Plym. The lines in and out of Plymstock, Oreston, Turnchapel and Yealmpton had long since ceased to transport passengers, but now, in the Seventies, came the end of any sort of rail link with the area that, from 1967 onwards, was now, officially, part of Plymouth.

Not that too many people noticed the difference. Each of the communities that made up the greater area of Plymstock, including Elburton, Hooe, and Goosewell, and all of the above, had their own village shops and if a more comprehensive shopping experience were needed then the Plymstock Broadway and the peripheral retail offer could satisfy most customers — so there was little need to venture into the big city.

Top: *King's Head and Ship's Tavern, Elburton.* Above: *Heading into the Laira Viaduct on a train, one of last opportunities for such a ride — October 1970.* Right: *Plymstock Broadway.*

Main image, plus inset and left on opposite page: *7 March 1978 Plymouth Co-operative Society's Plymco One opens on the Ridgeway.*
Top right: *Boxing legend, Henry Cooper, holding helium balloons, ably assisted by Andy Budge, at the opening of Plymco One.*

COME
CO·OPERATIVE
SHOPPING

For all the family

Similar sentiments prevailed in Plympton. Once again the constituent parts — Underlane, Colebrook, St Maurice and Ridgeway — all had their own small stores ... and pubs. As the Seventies dawned they didn't perhaps have anything quite as modern as the Broadway, but towards the middle of the decade the Plymouth and South West Devon Co-operative Society selected the Ridgeway as the place to build their first ever Superstore — Plymco One.

It was an instant success. Furthermore, the additional parking it created gave the whole of the Ridgeway a boost as a shopping centre. The following year, 1979, the Co-op bought Nos. 29-31 as a Pharmacy, and later that year they opened a freezer centre at the bottom of the Ridgeway with a ladies-hairdressing salon — Melanie — above it.

Around the same time the Society made a substantial investment in Bell Close, on the Newnham Industrial Estate, where they built a brand new food distribution centre. The facility opened in January 1978, just ahead of the superstore, which meant that the post-war four-storey grocery warehouse on North Quay was now surplus to requirements. So too was the antiquated wooden warehouse in Lower Street, just off North Quay. This timely move meant the Society had two sites that were ripe for redevelopment in an area that was already being considered for upmarket apartments.

The Plympton initiatives all helped breathe fresh life into the Ridgeway itself, a welcome move given the fact that, thankfully, the A38 no longer ran through the middle of it.

Top: *Seymour Road, Plympton, outside the school gate, with an Arthur Cooper off licence in the distance.* Bottom: *Looking over Merafield towards Woodford c.1970.*

139

The Plympton Bypass had been opened in 1971, although not without something of a last-ditch stand from the National Trust as the route ran through the Saltram Estate, which they had acquired in 1957.

Notwithstanding their protests, the new section of road opened and by 1974 the entire stretch of A38 between Exeter and Marsh Mills was dual carriageway. The final section, between the eastern end of the Plympton By-Pass and the dual-carriageway near the Lee Mill Trading Estate, was opened in August that year.

Three years later there were even greater celebrations when, on 27 May 1977, the Prime Minister, James Callaghan, ceremonially cut a ribbon to acknowledge the fact that the infamous Exeter Bypass had been bypassed, and there was now an unbroken dual-carriageway link between Plymouth and Scotland.

The only issue locally, of course, was that it stopped at Marsh Mills: there was no dual-carriageway from there to the Tamar Bridge or the Torpoint Ferry. In other words there was no major artery running through the City into Cornwall.

There was already a plan however, and it had been on the drawing board since before the war. Back then it had been very much a northern route around the top of the city, now that line was more or less right through the middle of Plymouth. The land had been protected from development — apart from a few post-war prefabs — since 1937 and now, at last, there was talk of making a start: but first there needed to be a public enquiry.

Above and top right: *Plympton Bypass c.1973.*

Above: *Marsh Mills c.1979.* Left: *Plympton Bypass, November 1971.*

North Road Station c.1973

TRAINS, PLANES AND AUTOMOBILES

Plymouth Station was, we were told, 'one of the most modern in the Western Region.

'As part of the InterCity rail network it is linked directly with London and has 12 trains a day travelling in each direction, with more in the summer': 226 miles in little more than three and a half hours, was the proud boast.

For the business community it was also worth pointing out that there was a Rail Express Parcels Service and a Freight Depot right in the City.

A large, window-free, canopied area stood at the entrance to the station and a limited number of parking bays backed up to it, allowing for a degree of unpacking without getting too wet in the event of rain.

Left: *North Road Station pre-1971 (4 photos for 2/6d).* Right: *Exterior shot from 1972.*

Brymon Airways, Plymouth Airport c.1973. Inset: *Prime Minister Edward Heath leaving Roborough, August 1971.*

There was even less protection afforded to air passengers at Plymouth Airport. There had been flying from the airfield at Roborough since 1931, and various operators had shown interest in running scheduled flights to and from the City, among them Dan Air and South West Aviation.

A London service had started up in 1971, but it wasn't until the arrival of Brymon Airways that Plymouth Airport really started to pick up.

Brymon was the brainchild of journalist Bill Bryce and 27-year-old Formula One racing driving Chris Amon — the trading name was an amalgam of parts of their surnames.

Although highly regarded in the profession, Chris Amon has been described as *'one of the best drivers never to win a championship Grand Prix'*, indeed such was his reputation for being unlucky that fellow F1 star, Mario Andretti once quipped that if Chris *'became an undertaker people would stop dying'*.

Undaunted, Bryce and Amon set up their business. Incorporated in January 1970 as Brymon Aviation Limited operating as Brymon Airways, Plymouth became their headquarters and Newquay a second base.

In 1972 they started regular services and before long built up a number of routes taking in the Channel Islands and the Isles of Scilly.

As the decade unfolded further destinations were added and the offer came to include regular winter and summer flights to Morlaix, Cherbourg and Cork.

In 1978 it was announced that Brymon had been given the go ahead to to fly to London (Gatwick) and the following year a new Plymouth to Birmingham service was inaugurated. A tourist delegation from the Midlands, led by Mr Swatman, vice-chairman of the Birmingham Airport Committee, was received by the Lord Mayor, Bill Evans, in the Mayoral Parlour before being taken to the Mayflower Post House, where they were wined and dined by the Plymouth Marketing Bureau.

Brymon, incidentally, also maintained an eight-seater aircraft that was available for private hire, while the airport itself was also used by charter, private and business executives' aircraft.

Top: *Boarding and on board South West Aviation's first flight out of Roborough to London, 6 July 1971, on a Short SC-7 Skyvan.* Bottom: *Brymon hostesses in their new uniforms, November 1976.*

It was, doubtless, no coincidence that, just a couple of weeks after South West Aviation had scheduled their first flight from Roborough to London, in July 1971, there was a major air show staged at the City Airport.

South West Aviation (SWA) had been formed in 1966, essentially to pick up air charter work from Exeter. Two years later they purchased a Short SC-7 Skyvan that enabled it to work out of small grass airfields and to operate a scheduled service between Plymouth and Heathrow. By 1970 they had a fleet of just four aircraft — the Skyvan, which could carry 21 passengers, plus two 21-seater Douglas DC-3s and a small 4-6-seater Piper Aztec.

The company was short-lived and in 1973 was apparently subsumed by Skyways Aviation.

The 1971 Air Show, meanwhile, was quite an impressive affair — it was by no means the first show the city had seen. Indeed the Plymouth Air Show was something of an annual event, it featured some high-profile, high-flying machines.

'An announcement came over the loudspeaker system saying something like "the whispering wind is on its way" and seconds later the Vulcan B2, the world's first large delta-wing bomber, which was capable of flying very high, or very low, beneath enemy radar, came flat across the airfield,' recalled John James later. *'My son, Steven, bent down to pick something up, and the Vulcan, flying at a high, subsonic speed, suddenly changed direction and went straight up in the air. Steven was knocked out by it, he literally fell flat on the ground in amazement!'* A few early jets and a Tempest display had also contributed to the afternoon's entertainment.

Amazingly enough there was little or no security on the airfield back then, apart from on Air Show days: *'Roborough was open to anyone to walk in on a day-to-day basis. You could wander around the field and in the hangars if you asked nicely,'* recounts Jim Warwick who was twelve and a member of the model aeroplane club in 1971. You could also book a pleasure flight over the City for ten shillings (50p).

In 1970, incidentally, as a link with the Mayflower celebrations, Maj-Gen John H Bell, commander of the Third United States Air Force in Europe was invited to open that year's show and the first on the programme was a fly-past by supersonic Phantom aircraft of the US 81st Tactical Fighter Wing.

Plymouth Air Show

Saturday, 24th July, 1971

City Airport Roborough, Plymouth

Official programme 10p

Opposite page: *A scheduled flight for the short-lived South West Aviation.* Inset: Top and Bottom right: *A Vulcan and two Super Sabres at the Plymouth Air Show.* Bottom left: *Watching a take-off.*

Castle Motor's Graham Flood's Series 2 Lamborghini Espada parked outside the service station in Exeter Street, note the section of Quadrophonic tapes on sale inside.

Just as air travel was becoming more and more affordable — and popular — in the Seventies, so too was motoring.

The number of private cars had been increasing enormously since the war and competition for customers had made the manufacturers more and more mindful of making improvements that might make the difference.

Pretty pin-up girls had been used to help make cars appear more sexy since the Sixties, but there were a number of other elements in the equation that saw massive swings in the industry.

The introduction of the hatchback had a huge impact on design and use, as did any number of improvements in softening the interior, making it warmer, quieter and more comfortable.

Previously it had been the lot of the luxury car to have such refinements — roof linings, boot linings, carpets, comfy seats and door trim etc., but now these features were coming as standard.

Reliability too made a difference, and throughout the decade the foreign car manufacturers, especially the Japanese, made massive inroads into the British market.

The introduction of the audio casette also transformed the in-car experience, especially now cars were quieter. People could control their travel time more effectively than ever before. Small wonder that public transport suffered from falling numbers.

The Government, however, was aware of the situation and put pressure on local authorities to find solutions to the various issues raised. The first big one, with more cars than ever on the road, was the safety of pedestrians.

In 1971 specifications for traffic lights were changed: grey poles replaced their black-and-white predecessors, while high-intensity tungsten halogen lamps were introduced in place of tungsten filaments. Furthermore they were set in a black head with a white border and, by all accounts, had an almost immediate impact on the number of accidents.

That same year it was decided that there should be zig-zag markings on either side of zebra crossings to indicate no waiting or parking areas. The following year another safety initiative saw Plymouth's first Pelican crossing (PEdestrian LIght CONtrolled) installed — in Notte Street.

The Seventies also witnessed the introduction into Plymouth of special bus lanes, part of a Devon County Council-inspired drive to assist the ailing bus industry.

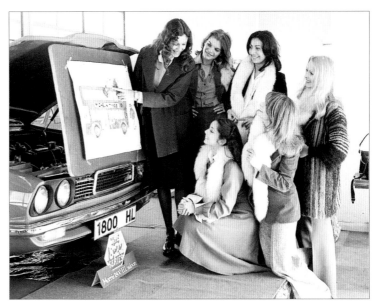

Top: *1975, Pan's People, those Top of the Pops dancers, dad's favourites across the country, visiting Mumford's in Plymouth for the launch of the new Austin Morris 18/22 range, with, possibly, Flick Colby, Dee Dee Wilde (back row), with Ruth Pearson, Louise Clarke, Sue Menhenick and Cherry Gillespie (front). Bottom: 1971 — new zigzag lines either side of zebra crossings introduced.*

SCHOOLDAYS

At the beginning of the Seventies there were some 74 primary schools for infants and juniors 'situated conveniently to serve the residential areas of the City' with a further 15 providing denominational education for children of the Church of England and Roman Catholic faiths. As the decade progressed two more were added to the former total and one removed from the latter.

For children of secondary school age there were 33 schools throughout the City, ten of which were selective entry grammar schools and there was an element of streaming in the two comprehensive schools..

Of the two comprehensives Southway was the oldest, having been been opened in 1962 with the Swiss-born Peter Bindschedler as its head — he was there throughout the Sixties and the Seventies, as were two members of staff, Diane Evans and John Ellis.

As the Southway estate grew — it became a parish in its own right in 1971 — so too did the school, and before long it had become one of the biggest schools in the City.

It's interesting to note that the local authority described the other schools as offering *a good modern secondary education, including three which provide denominational education for children of the Church of England or the Roman Catholic faith'.*

Opposite page: Headmaster Peter Bindschedler handing out humane awards at Southway Comprehensive, April 1971. Above: Southway Comp. Right: Soutway staff, including: Don Reby, Di Evans, Phil Arscott, Peter Bindschedler, Reg Hambly, Ralph Broom, Ron Furness, Henry Taylor, Betty Saunders, Des Robinson, John Ellis, Harry Cook, Rex James and Larry Hawkridge.

Plymstock Comprehensive School cross-country race 23 January 1971.

Plymouth's other comprehensive school at the start of the Seventies was Plymstock. Much the older of the two institutions in some respects, it had opened in 1911 as Plymstock Senior Mixed School, later becoming Plymstock County Mixed, the County Secondary School, before being re-invented as a Comprehensive in 1965.

The new designation saw a significant increase in numbers and in 1969/70 the campus was extended and new buildings added so that a further 300 pupils could be accommodated.

When Clifford Hands arrived as the new headteacher in 1974 numbers were heading for an all-time peak of around 2,300, making it one of the largest in Western Europe.

Certainly the high numbers gave it the opportunity to offer pupils a wide range of academic subjects and sporting options.

In 1976 one of their pupils hit the headlines as 13-year-old Sharron Davies became the youngest member of the British swimming team for that year's Olympic Games being held in Montreal. She didn't end up with a medal that time, but the following year she picked up two bronze medals in the European Championships and in 1978 she struck gold in Commonwealth games.

Sharon Davies (left) at her desk in Plymstock School.

Top: *Plymstock v Hele's School, March 1971.* Bottom: *Plymstock gymnasts, 1974.*

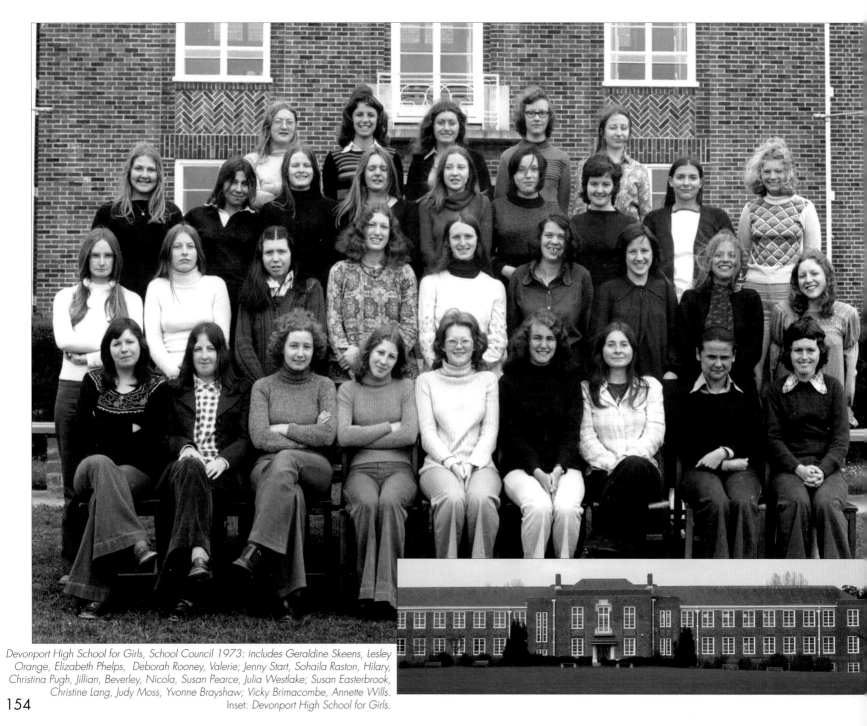

Devonport High School for Girls, School Council 1973: includes Geraldine Skeens, Lesley Orange, Elizabeth Phelps, Deborah Rooney, Valerie; Jenny Start, Sohaila Raston, Hilary, Christina Pugh, Jillian, Beverley, Nicola, Susan Pearce, Julia Westlake; Susan Easterbrook, Christine Lang, Judy Moss, Yvonne Brayshaw; Vicky Brimacombe, Annette Wills. Inset: Devonport High School for Girls.

Plymouth's ten grammar schools in the Seventies were mainly single-sex affairs and included: Devonport High School for Girls, Devonport High School for Boys, Plymouth High School for Girls, Stoke Damerel High School for Girls, Sutton High School for Boys, Public, and Plympton Grammar, which was mixed, as indeed was Tamar, from 1972.

The then Deputy Head, Ray Rose, later noted that *'staff, who had been accustomed to teaching boys only, soon realised that any misgivings they might have had were unfounded: indeed many thought their lessons in the first year were enhanced, and perhaps more successful with the added presence and competitive atmosphere brought about by the girls. The girls themselves showed few signs of being overawed by the fact that they were outnumbered by ten to one.'*

Someone who was definitely not overawed by any kind of adversity was one of Tamar's star pupils at the time, Tony Willis. Having had the handicap of losing a leg at the age of eight, Tony *'won places, on merit, in school basketball, football, cricket and athletics teams'*. His most notable success came in the high jump: representing Devon, he competed at four National Schools Athletic Championships and 1970/71 came joint second at Crystal Palace. In 1974 he went to Marjons to train as a PE teacher and by the end of the decade had a teaching post in Plymouth.

Tamar had a number of changes at the top in the early Seventies, Dr Rowe, who had only become head in 1968 moved on to Sutton High School in 1971, whereupon stalwart staff member HWA Warren became acting head, until retiring, after 41 years' service in December 1972. His successor was Mr F Hill DFC.

There were changes at the top, too, at Devonport High School for Girls, when Mrs Audrey Clayton became the first ever married headmistress of that institution after more than 60 years.

Meanwhile, Miss Doris Dixon was the head at Stoke Damerel High School for Girls from 1959-79 and was followed by Maureen Green, who became SDHS's first married head. At Plymouth High for Girls, Muriel Newman succeeded Margaret Farrar. Miss Farrar, incidentally, had waived the wearing of uniform in the 6th Form.

Top left: Tony Willis. Top right: *Tamar School, off Stonehouse Creek before creek infilled.* Above left: *DHSG Speech Day in the Guildhall, 1974 — Susan Pearce, Jenny Start, Geraldine Skeens, Annette Wills, Judy Moss.* Above right: *SDHSG 1977 staff: back row; Mr Childs, anon, Mr Goode, Mr Jones, Mr Rowe, Mr Montague, Mr Blatt, Mr Liddicoat, Mr Clarke, Mr Screech. Middle: Mrs Cartwright, Miss Slack, Mrs Merret, anon, Miss Neno, anon, Mrs Hough, Mrs Morgan, Mrs Liddell, anon, Mrs Trenerry. Front: Mrs Southern, Mrs Arnold, Mrs Warne, Miss Causley, Miss Squire, Miss Dixon, Mrs Markham, Miss Rashbrook, Miss Cann, Mrs Bullock, Mrs Kelly.*

Muriel Newman, for her part, decided that, at Plymouth High, the school hat had had its day. Certainly across the City and across the country, a lot of traditions were being cast aside at a seemingly alarming rate.

Pupils increasingly were tweaking their uniform, boys' ties were tied shorter, colourful socks flashed between grey trousers and black shoes while girls' skirts got shorter, and shorter.

Meanwhile, if sartorial standards were slipping somewhat in the classroom, in the common room there was mounting disquiet among many teachers about behaviour.

Henry Whitfeld, very much a traditionalist, who started teaching English at his old school, Devonport High for Boys, in 1934, and who finally retired in 1969, was an outspoken critic of the comprehensive system which was starting to impact at that time in Plymouth.

He saw large 1,500-2,000 establishments as *'child factories'* where *'anonymity was inevitable, leading to resentment by pupils, and the subordination of the individual to the gang and of the introvert, diffident and unsure, to the self-confident extrovert and bully'.*

He cited an example of a young girl his wife encountered at a local private school. The girl had been moved from a large comprehensive where she had been labelled *'unteachable'.* However it transpired that she behaved perfectly normally in her new school and when discreetly asked why, she replied that there hadn't been anyone at the previous school who *'knew or valued me as a person, I was just an object'.*

Around the same time Whitfeld cited the story of a young student teacher who turned up at DHS on teaching practice and then got a full-time post at a local comprehensive.

'Some time later I met him in Plymouth and asked him how he was getting on. "I'm most unhappy," he replied, "I don't think the Head of my Department has found out yet that I am on the staff and the classroom teaching is a nightmare." Shortly after this, I heard that he had committed suicide.'

There was no doubt that the situation in the classroom had deteriorated. Whitfeld painted a particularly bleak picture of it: *'violence, vandalism and gross insubordination became a feature of our "blackboard jungles" as the Seventies progressed.'*

At Plymouth College your author recalls one pupil being expelled for pinning a teacher against a wall and telling him to 'f***-off' in the middle of a lesson. The pupil was expelled and subsequently went to DHS ... and then as fate would have it, he became a teacher and later a headmaster.

Top: *Sutton High School football team 1972/3 Front: Dr Rowe (headmaster), Derek Sowden, Ian Trethowan, Wayne Brelsford, Kenny Reed, Mr Lambert (teacher) Back Row Steve Ladlow, Steve Downing, Phil Thomas and Rob B. Bottom: DHS for Boys, Sports Day, 1971.*

March 1972, Devonport High School for Boys (Charles Evans far right) play a Canadian touring team.

Plymouth College itself expanded somewhat in the early Seventies, building a new assembly hall and separate geography, technology and sixth-form common-room block.

The new hall was named the Meade-King Hall in honour of the headmaster, Martin Meade-King, who retired in 1973 after 18 years in the hot seat, making him the second longest-serving head since the school had been founded in 1877. By contrast his successor, John Goddard, was one of the school's shortest-serving heads and left inside two years, having perhaps tried to do too much too quickly, alienating the common-room in the process.

Thus it was that Ron Merrett became the twelfth head and was in post to host the school's centenary. He was also there to witness one of the first theatrical appearances of young Michael Ball, who, much to the discomfort of the aforementioned Mr Merrett, opted to drop down from the stage during the Christmas Entertainment and serenade the headmaster while sitting on his lap.

The Seventies also saw the gradual introduction of girls into the sixth form of Plymouth College, but a little too late for Seventies Plymouth schoolgirl, Dawn French. Dawn's brother, Gary was a pupil at the college, while Dawn was a boarder at what was then the City's only surviving independent school for girls, St Dunstan's Abbey in North Road West.

The two establishments got on well together and Dawn and her chums regularly, on a Friday after school, made *'a 30-minute brisk lug up North Road, past the train station, over the top of Pennycomequick, on to the bottom of Mutley Plain and into Goodbody's coffee shop. There they were, the pantheon of prized Plymouth College sixth-formers, all sitting at one table huddled around hot chocolates. Bliss.'*

Top left: *Plymouth College 1st XI 1971: GP Lawrence (scorer) Simon Murray, David Bryant, Chris Wood, Patrick Marsh, Mike Warren. Nick Bridge. Front: Kingsley Bishop, Keith Johnson, Ian Smith, John Martin, Nigel Baxter.*
Left: *Plymouth College outdoor swimming pool.* Above: *Sports day 1971, Brickfields.*

Above: *Plymouth College — Heamaster Martin Meade-King takes the school assembly. c.1971.*
Far left: *The new Meade-King Hall, 1974.*
Left: *Teachers, Keith Dockray, Doug Martin, Dennis Collinson and Ivor Cleaves in the staff/pupil Christmas production of 'The Happiest Days of Your Life'.*

It was on stage at St Dunstan's that Dawn made one of her first acting appearances, in the school's production of Tim Rice and Andrew Lloyd Webber's 'Joseph and His Technicolour Dreamcoat'.

Plymouth College had been originally founded as Plymouth High School for Boys, and it was essentially the same group of local churchmen and worthies who had, a year earlier, set up Plymouth High School for Girls, at the other end of Mutley Plain, at the top of North Hill.

The other selective-entry schools around at the time included two schools that were essentially separate, but in fact were on one site occupying different parts of the same building: Public School had a boys' and girls' section: television journalist Angela Rippon was a well-known pupil at the latter, while footballer Trevor Francis left the boys' school as a 16-year-old in 1970. Trevor's father had never wanted him to sign for Argyle and that summer he signed for First Division Birmingham City. In his first season he scored 15 goals in 22 games, including four against Bolton when he was still just 16.

In 1977 he was given his first England cap by Don Revie and two years later he became the stuff of football legends by signing for Brian Clough and moving to Nottingham Forest for over a million pounds — the first player ever to move between English clubs for a seven-figure fee.

Another Seventies selective-entry establishment was Widey Tech, the alumnus of the actor Charles Dance. However, the changing educational landscape of the City meant that the venerable institution struggled throughout the decade.

St Boniface College, also had its share of difficulties in the Seventies. Following the decision of the Labour Government to withdraw funding from direct-grant schools in 1976, 'Bonnies' opted to become an independent school, but it didn't really work out and towards the end of the decade they looked to amalgamate with the City's other Catholic Boy's School, Bishop Vaughan, at Manadon.

Interestingly enough, its sister school, Notre Dame, at Derriford, was one of 51 (out of 170) Direct Grant schools that opted instead to go comprehensive in 1976.

Top: *Dawn French and chums, Nicky and Nicky, in St Dunstan's summer attire.* Bottom: *St Dunstan's U16 Hockey League winners 1971, includes (back row), Lorna Paige, Sharon, Helen Fraser, (front), Jan Blackaller, Jinny Hales, Gillian Weeks, Peggy Quayle, Sharon, Rosemary Courtney.*

Top left: *St Boniface College teacher Keith Maddox (former Welsh International) with the school first XI which includes Kevin Norris*. Top right: *Plymouth High School for Girls netball squad, includes Jane Maddox*. Above left: *Plymouth 12th Girl Guides troupe tennis team at Plympton Grammar School*. Above right: *Public Secondary School for Girls, Sports Day, 1971.*

While more schools were going down the comprehensive route as the Seventies progressed, the tendency was for them to be slightly smaller than some of the larger and more daunting establishments that appeared in the first flush of comprehensive excitement.

The critics though, were still sceptical, particularly as some of the comprehensives started thinking about streaming, a move some saw as counter intuitive.

'If the pupils were streamed, then the prime motive in the change — social and ability mixing — would be completely defeated. Obviously it would be far more discouraging to be in a Comprehensive 'N' stream than a Secondary Modern 'C' stream. If, however,' reasoned Kim Taylor in his articulate and hugely influential tome, *Resources for Learning,* published by Penguin in 1971, *'there was to be no streaming, classroom teaching in the traditional sense was manifestly impossible ...'*

Of course traditional teaching was rapidly becoming a thing of the past, a blackboard and a piece of chalk was no longer sufficient armoury for the modern teacher, as Taylor observed: *'some teachers now add, from time to time, broadcasts, records, slides, film-loops, overhead-projector transparencies and films. Indeed the modern teacher, as he emerges in conferences and in articles, is expected to achieve prodigies of co-ordination, busking his restive audience like a one-man band.'*

Mr Taylor however, was not a fan: *' "Chalk and talk" and book may be less vivid, but they are also less obtrusive and less complicated to set up; they allow quick response to mood and they do not break down at the most maddening and embarrassing moments'.*

Above: The 'chalk and talk' generation with George Bonser teaching further maths at Plymouth College and (above right) Ted Mercer, another Plymouth College maths master and well-known local rugby enthusiast.

Les Thomas taking a chemistry class at St Boniface College. Inset: Lord Mayor, Dorothy Innes makes a visit to Public Secondary School for Girls, March 1971.

Whatever the state of the latest technologies there was, undoubtedly, still a place for the book in the classroom and new libraries were opened across the City. Television, however, was, slowly but surely, tightening its grip on the minds of the nation's young people.

Watch With Mother and shows like *Blue Peter*, *Crackerjack* and *Vision On* were already well-established, but the Seventies saw a massive increase in the output aimed at children.

No sooner had the Government eased restrictions of broadcasting hours, notably around off-peak times when all that was on offer was the test card, than Britain's only two television providers, the BBC and ITV started producing a whole range of new material.

At the start of the decade the average weekly regional ITV children's fare was about seven hours. In 1972 the broadcaster was allowed to open up daytime TV and began a half-hour slot around midday devoted to pre-school children.

Rainbow was first scheduled that year and *Pipkins* hit the screen the following year.

In the meantime the BBC had commissioned *Crystal Tipps and Alistair*, *Mr Benn* (which David McKee created in Plymouth), *Play Away* (in 1971) and *Fingerbobs* (in 1972).

Oddly enough it was a while before non-school days were seriously targeted. In 1972 *Saturday Scene*, a London ITV initiative, became the children's show to be screened on a Saturday morning, the Midlands-based *TISWAS (Today Is Saturday Wear A Smile)* gaining universal exposure two years later.

The BBC had flirted with Saturday lunchtime output, *Edandzed!* (1970) and *Outa-Space* (1973), before mounting a serious challenge

to *TISWAS* with Noel Edmonds and the *Multi-Coloured Swap Shop* in 1976. The title being an indication of another element in the medium's growing success — television had gone colour! At midnight on 15 November 1969, BBC 1 and ITV simultaneously caught up with BBC2 which had been transmitting via 625-lines on UHF since 1967.

By the end of the Seventies the degree to which the genre had grown up was epitomised by a gritty new BBC offering *Grange Hill*, a far from cosy or rosy portrayal of school life that wasn't afraid to pull uncomfortable punches. But to what extent was it a case of art imitating life or art impacting on the everyday?

Either way, the amount of teen-targeted television, and younger, escalated, putting pressure on teachers who had little of the technical wizardry afforded by television presenters. It also provided an arguably less-than-healthy alternative to outdoor pursuits like climbing trees, playing football, scouting, guiding and all manner of other traditional, social pastimes.

Of course it didn't kill them off altogether, there was still a healthy appetite for such activities. In July 1976, the Diamond Jubilee of the Cub Scout Movement was celebrated locally with its own 'Olympic' Games.

Bickleigh Vale, not Montreal, was the chosen location and a total of 42 different cub packs provided a total of over 1,100 cubs, many of them dressed in national costume.

Lord Mayor Arthur Floyd started the ball rolling, or at least the Olympic torch moving, having handed on to the first of many torch-bearers at Blindman's Wood, and, at Bickleigh, local television personality, Gus Honeybun, was on hand to light the Olympic flame.

Top: *A new children's library opens in Plymstock, 1971.* Middle: *Stuart Road Primary School football team 1970: Back: Mr Thorogood, Richard Sanders, Andy lowe, Andrew Moore, Nick Hellings, David Trennery, Philip Thomas, Mr O'Gara. Front: Colin Astley, Chris Bunney, Chris Woodward, Adrian 'Acky' Cause, Richard 'FP' Palmer.* Bottom: *Montpelier lads playing football at Barn Park, 1971.*

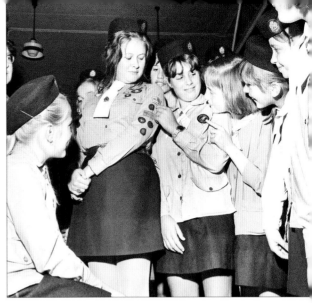

Clockwise from top: Ernie Cross is made an honorary member of the Southway Scouts, 1971; Cubs at Blindman's Wood, 1976; Queen's Award Presentation, Eggbuckland Guides, 1971; 23rd Plymouth Methodist Central Hall Brownies, 1972; Scout races on the Hoe, 1975; Gus Honeybun lights the Olympic torch at Blindman's Wood, 1976.

Notwithstanding the lure of the television, Youth Clubs were still a vital part of the social fabric.

In 1961, following the panic in the press that had been fanned in the fifties by the flames of rock'n'roll raising concerns over teenage rebels and juvenile delinquency, the National Association of Youth Clubs had been put together as an umbrella for earlier organisations. A government paper — the Albemarle Report — was published which led to the birth of the statutory sector of the youth service introducing, for the first time, youth centres and full-time, fully-paid youth workers.

Following the publication, five years later, of the National Association's report 'The Unattached', more funding became available, and record-players, table-tennis tables, pool tables, tables and chairs, other affordable pieces of furniture and equipment were purchased. They were installed in huts and halls the across the country and, of course, across the City of Plymouth in an attempt to improve the lot, and the behaviour of the young. Also, perhaps steer them toward more worthy pursuits.

Top left: *Southway Comprehensive School Common Room, 1979.* Above left and right: *1971 Coxside Youth Centre, St Gabriel's Youth Club.*

1971 Southway Youth Club.

FURTHER EDUCATION

The availability of further education opportunities in the Plymouth area increased dramatically in the Seventies as the old Technical College was upgraded, enhanced and transformed into a Polytechnic; a brand new Art College building was erected at the top of Charles Street, across from the Polytechnic and below the Central Library; a substantial new College of Further Education was built on the site of King's Road Station, Devonport, and, on the northern fringes of the City, a site was cleared and developed to accommodate the incoming teacher-training facility, the College of St Mark and St John.

Marjons, as the St Mark and St John establishment was affectionately known, was actually the result of the amalgamation, in 1926, of two earlier London establishments: St Mark's and St John's. The latter had been founded by Dr James Phillips Kay in 1840, in Battersea, while the former owed its origins to Reverend Derwent Coleridge (son of Samuel Taylor Coleridge) who set up stall in Chelsea the following year.

Coleridge's ethos and primary purpose was based around giving his students as broad an education as possible.

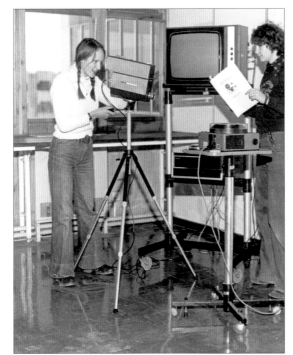 

Opposite page: *November 1972, work progresses on A & B Block at the new College of St Mark and St John.*
Above left and right: *Marjon's new TV studio and language laboratory.*

*The campus starts to ta take shape. Inset: An early football match on the site.
Opposite page top: Marjons canteen. Bottom: A student bar. Left: In the gym.*

Based in the St Mark's site in King's Road, Chelsea, since their amalgamation, they had been forced to vacate their home in the capital following the decision, in the late Sixties, to create an Inner London Motorway. So it was that an 'advanced post' arrived in Devonport in 1969, initially to provide two-year courses for mature students returning to, or taking up, work in primary schools. Four years later the Roborough/Derriford campus was ready for occupation.

With its sports grounds and halls, function spaces and bars, the college was a welcome addition to the local education scene and, with its strong emphasis on international recruitment, it brought a colourful element into the community. Socially, culturally, and commercially the move was hailed as *'a big advance in the City's educational facilities and as such was an important boost for its economy.'*

Another boost came as a consequence of the former Tech College being re-designated as a Polytechnic. The School of Architecture was hived off from the College of Art and Design and given a separate identity. At the same time approval was given to construct a new College of Art and Design on what had been Park Street — where the original Plymouth Drawing School had started more than 100 years earlier.

Plymouth's original School of Art had had various locations around and about — Cobourg Street, the erstwhile Park Street and Ebrington Street — none of them more than a hundred yards or so from the new site, before finally, in 1892, it became part of the Jubilee Memorial Science, Art and Technical School in Tavistock Road.

That building became a victim of post-war redevelopment some seventy or so years later, but it had long since ceased to house the Plymouth College of Arts and Crafts which, by then, had relocated to the former Palace Court School premises.

The all-new, five-storey building in Park Street was designed by City Architect Hector Stirling and was officially opened on 29 March 1974 – the cost being around £300,000. Meanwhile, the School of Architecture hopped around various old art college locations — Portland Square, Palace Court, Virginia House and Martin's Gate — before settling in the former NAAFI building in Notte Street, which was then re-styled 'The Hoe Centre'.

Top left: *The site is cleared c.1970.* Middle: *Building work under way c.1972*
Bottom: *Nearing completion, looking west c.1973.* Above: *Almost finished.*

Plymouth College of Art and Design soon after completion in 1974.

Across the road from the new Art College the newly created Polytechnic, one of 30 such re-designations around the country, marked a clear step change in Plymouth's Further Education provision. The ramifications went well beyond simply changing the neon sign on the college hall from College of Technology to Plymouth Polytechnic.

The main eight-storey block and the Poly Main Hall that extended from it, had been opened in March 1967, a year after the notion that this might become a Polytechnic had first been floated. The ten-storey Residential Nautical College, part of the Faculty of Maritime Studies, was opened in 1970, along with an adjoining teaching block and planetarium.

The accommodation block, replete with dining rooms, common rooms and study rooms, housed a potential 200 cadets. Overall there were a total of 1,207 students enrolled at the Polytechnic in 1970 (of whom 459 were undergraduates) but that number grew through the Seventies and by the end of the decade there were some 3,000 full-time equivalent students.

Another event that year saw the Polytechnic make its contribution to the Mayflower '70 programme. The Captain-Superintendent of the United States Merchant Marine Academy King's Point, New York, was invited to be guest of honour at the School of Maritime Studies' Mayflower Ball. Entertainment was provided by Bob Miller and the Millermen, with support from Rod Mason and the Tamar Valley Jazz Band.

The Maritime School project was one of a number of schemes that came to fruition on the expanding campus in the Seventies: 1976 saw the completion of the Library, Learning Resources Centre and Student Union.

Top: *Plymouth Polytechnic.* Bottom: *The School of Maritme Studies c.1973.*

Above: *Poly students playing football, March 1971.* Opposite page: *Rag Week, 1972.*

In the Sixties, the old Devonport Technical College had been functioning as part of Plymouth Technical College, but now, with the new Polytechnic providing higher education degree and diploma courses for students of 18 and over, it meant that there was a large amount of less advanced work uncovered in the City, hence the move to set up the College of Further Education.

Established in 1970, the same year as the Poly was formally constituted, the CFE (as it was inevitably abbreviated to), initially operated from more than 15 annexes dotted all over Plymouth — among them, some of the electrical and engineering areas of the Polytechnic and the Dockyard Apprentice Training Centre.

In the event, it was not until September 1974 that the major part of the new development on the former King's Road railway station was completed.

Administered and organised completely independently of the Polytechnic, the new development wasn't initially big enough to house all of the departments and a few annexes continued to operate, most notably the College of Domestic Science (which had merged with the CFE in 1973) in small, rundown premises in Portland Square, and the old Devonport Tech building itself, which was home to the Commerce and Business Studies Department.

Phase two of the King's Road development was completed in 1975, but even then 60% of the teaching and the work of the College was carried on, off-site, often in premises that were in poor condition, prone to the ingress of rain and heating breakdowns.

Nevertheless numbers grew and by the end of the decade there were over 10,000 students enrolled, of whom nearly 2,500 were on full-time or sandwich courses, and 3,773 'on release' from local industry for 'full part time day or part time day/evening courses'.

Left, top and bottom: *The last traces of the railway in and out of King's Road are rapidly disappearing as the new College takes shape.*

The new College of Further Education, opened on King's Road site in 1974.

A 1970 Plymouth wedding. Drummer Ray Mitchell and hair-stylist Mary Paul tie the knot with members of the band Chimera in attendance. The band for a while worked as Long John Baldry's backing band — Long John is the tall one, on the other side of the bride, he was 6'7".

SOCIAL LIFE

If the Sixties had been the decade in which men started to grow their hair really quite long, the early Seventies witnessed a truly androgenous approach to style and fashion on behalf of many men and a fair few women.

In the wake of Beatlemania boys had already begun to let their hair down, but now David Bowie, Marc Bolan and a wave of fellow Glam Rockers, were introducing mascara and a little bit of lipstick into the range of options, along with leotards, leggings, elevating footwear and earrings.

In response, girls started wearing the trousers more often than ever before: trousers ... and jeans and, at the other end of the spectrum entirely, very, very short trousers that were christened 'Hot Pants'.

Exposing even more leg than the mini skirt had in the Sixties, they didn't suit all those who invested in them and, as fashion fads go, they were relatively short-lived.

But it was an era in which the pendulum swung so far in favour of the exposure of flesh, and semi-smutty seaside postcard humour (a la Benny Hill and Frankie Howerd), that there was bound to be a reaction, and so the midi-skirt was followed swiftly by the maxi — and then came punk.

Boys on a night out, in 1972 — the Old Public Oaks rugby team scrub up well.

A Seventies fashion shoot for Dingles.

179

Miss Mayflower '70 Sandra Ann Ritchie, promoting Watney's Red Barrell in a local pub.

Notwithstanding all these changes though, the annual stripping off of clothes in pursuit of a sash bearing the words Miss fill-in-the-blank, fill-in-the-year appeared to be as popular as ever.

Miss Mayflower '70, 22-year-old Sandra Ann Ritchie, was, undoubtedly, one of the hardest worked locally, opening events and appearing at various functions throughout her year in office. Sandra also won the Miss Westward title and, on at least one occasion, was persuaded to promote one of those beers that was indirectly responsible for the foundation, in 1971, of the Campaign for Real Ale — Watneys Red Barrel.

Meanwhile, at the other end of the decade, 18-year-old Carolyn Seaward, from Yelverton, won the Miss England and Miss United Kingdom titles in 1979. Then, later in the year, as Miss England, Carolyn was entered into Miss Universe where she came third. Although there didn't appear to be any entrants from any planet other than this one, the title was separate and distinct from the Miss World competition, a beauty parade she was able to enter in her capacity as Miss United Kingdom. This time she came second, pipped at the post by Bermudan beauty Gina Swainson, who had been second in the Miss Universe contest.

Clockwise from top left: A selection of other local beauties; the Co-op's 1978 Miss Dairy Queen; Argyle's Miss Plymouth 1970, Toni Marie German, with Robert Daniel and Ellis Studdard; Sandra Bradbury, Miss Berketex. 1971; Wendy Carter, Miss Meet the Marines and Carolyn Seaward, Miss England, in the Tecalemit nipple assembly department, 1979.

It would be a mistake, however, to assume that the Seventies was defined by events like these, rather the decade was one of profound change regarding the role of women in society — right across the world and across many aspects of culture.

There were, undoubtedly, more scantily clad women on television and in the media generally. Rupert Murdoch had relaunched the flagging *Sun* newspaper as a tabloid in November 1969 with a provocative image of that month's Penthouse Pet, Ulla Lindstrom in a see-through top on page three.

The following November, to mark the first birthday of Murdoch's reign, Stephanie Kahn appeared on the page, in her birthday suit, which was revealing, but not totally revealing, unlike some of the top-shelf magazines of the day, which increasingly, as the decade progressed, left less and less to the imagination.

But at the same time as this was happening the feminist movement that had started in the Sixties was gaining momentum.

Although it wasn't a major breakthrough, it was, nonetheless, a significant move when, in 1970, the BBC appointed Anne Nightingale as the first female disc jockey on Radio 1. That same year in the States there was the Women's Strike for Equality and in 1975, the year hailed as International Women's Year, both the Sex Discrimination Act and the Equal Pay Act came into force in the UK.

The previous year, interestingly enough, had seen Isabel Martinez Peron become the first female, non-royal, head of state in the Western World, when she took office as President in Argentina. It was also in 1975 that 50-year-old Margaret Thatcher was elected leader of the Conservatives, which paved the way for her becoming Britain's first female Prime Minister.

Top left: *Ladies Keep Fit in the Guildhall 1977.* Bottom: *Town Clerk's Office Keep Fit in the Council House.* Above: *Margaret Thatcher in Plymouth Pannier Market.*
Opposite page: *A fashion show, with 28-year-old local TV personality Angela Rippon, in the Holiday Inn, 1972.*

Clockwise from top left: *London Inn, Union Street, 1971; the NAAFI Tavern, Notte Street: the Seven Stars beer garden, 1977; inside the Hyde Park Hotel, 1975; Lord Roborough in the Lopes Arms, 1971; Beacon Park Social Club, 1970.*

The times certainly were 'a-changing' but although people appeared to have more freedom in many different aspects of life, the time they could visit their local licensed premises had changed little since the Defence of the Realm restrictions had been brought in during the First World War.

Pubs were permitted to open at 10 o'clock in the morning, but the landlord had to call time at 2.30pm and then wasn't allowed to pull another pint until 6pm. Last orders had to be served by 10.30pm most of the year, apart from the summer months when there was an extension lasting through until 11pm. The 11 o'clock curfew also applied to Friday and Saturday nights, all year round.

Sundays were different again: doors couldn't open until midday and were closed again after time had been called at 2pm. The evening session on Sundays was similarly truncated, as landlords were not permitted to admit customers before 7 o'clock.

Late-night drinking was restricted to night clubs, of which there were but a few, most of which had integral discotheques and could stay open until 2am, if they had a hot food provision available.

Most areas had their own off-licences within easy reach and among the popular party fare you could buy were Watney's Party Sevens — massive seven-pint tins of fizzy keg. Alternatively, if you were a little more sophisticated, perhaps a bottle of Blue Nun, Black Tower, Hock, Liebfraumilch, or if you were pushing the boat out — Mateus Rosé. Martini ('any time, any place, any where'), Cinzano and Advocat- based Snowballs were also popular, particularly with the ladies.

In pubs themselves, the early Seventies was the 'golden' age of keg bitter. Watney's Red Barrel, Double Diamond, and Worthington 'E' were popular with many, but by no means all, hence the rise of 'Euro-fizz': lager, particularly Carling Black Label, Harp, Skol and, on the stronger side, Stella Artois, were gaining a foothold in British pubs, Hence the growing popularity of CAMRA, the Campaign for Real Ale, founded in 1971. In 1978, the Swan, in Devonport, became one of the first, local, real-ale pubs.

Clockwise from top left: The Lockyer Tavern; Talbot Hotel, Union Street; The Star, Union Street; Royal Albert Bridge Inn, Saltash Passage, the Hyde Park, and the Thistle Park Tavern.

ABC CINEMA PLYMOUTH

FRIDAY 22nd JUNE

at 7.45 p.m.

FREDERICK BANNISTER

In association with

ROBERT STIGWOOD

PRESENTS

THE BEE GEES

ON TOUR

with 15 piece Orchestra

conducted by GLYN HALE

with ALAN KENDALL—lead guitar

and DENNIS BYRON—drums

supporting artiste JIMMY STEVENS

TICKETS : £1.50, £1.25, £1.00, 75p

DRAKE and ODEON

PLYMOUTH —— 68825

PROUDLY PRESENT FOR YOUR SUMMER
ENTERTAINMENT

ROGER MOORE as JAMES 007 BOND

THE SPY WHO LOVED ME (A)

AN ALL STAR CAST IN

A BRIDGE TOO FAR (A)

THE NEW SINBAD FILM

EYE OF THE TIGER (A)

WALT DISNEY'S

CINDERELLA (U)

WALT DISNEY'S

SHAGGY D.A. (U)

All coming your way this summer

1971, the Drake Cinema at the top of Union Strete, the Dad's Army Feature Film is 'now showing'. Inset various posters and advertisements.

Plymouth at one time had 17 separate cinemas. At the start of the Seventies the city had seven: the Drake, the ABC, the Odeon, the State (St Budeaux), the Belgrave (Mutley), Studio Seven and, tenuously, the Arts Centre.

By the end of the decade there were more screens, but across slightly fewer cinemas, with the closure of the State early in the decade and the Odeon at the end of it. Meanwhile, both the Drake and the ABC had gone triple-screen.

The change was effected at the Drake first, in 1975. Alex Greig, an affable Scot, was the manager at the time. The main screen retained a sort of upstairs/downstairs element. The upper area, being quite a small affair, was restyled 'the Luxury Lounge' and had space for placing drinks and snacks beside each pair of comfy seats. The Drake, incidentally, was where all of the James Bond films were first screened locally.

The transformation of the neighbouring ABC came two years later. Clive Jones was the genial general manager who took on the new three-screen cinema in May 1977 when the new split-screen and bingo-in-the-basement facility opened in the shell of the original William Riddle Glenn-designed building. One of the few major entertainment emporiums to have survived the Blitz, the ABC, with its 2,500 capacity, had been one of the City's main entertainment venues after the war, particularly after the old Regent (later Odeon) in New George Street had been pulled down. Thus it was here that the Beatles and the Rolling Stones played in the Sixties and here that the Bee Gees and the Bay City Rollers played in the Seventies. The latter gig resulting in the treatment of around 100 girls aged between 10-15 for hysteria, shock and minor injuries.

In the event it was Britain's favourite comedy duo Morecombe and Wise who were the last to appear live at the venue, while the final single-screen films to be shown there were two TV spin-off movies — *The Likely Lads* and *Steptoe and Son*. Remarkably, the assistant manager, Eileen Donovan, witnessed all of the events listed above as she had been one of the original staff members taken on when the cinema opened, on the site of the original Theatre Royal, in 1938. She was still there at the end of the Seventies.

Of the other cinemas, Studio Seven, which for much of the decade featured specialist films, mostly x-rated, was re-branded as the Plaza, its original name, when new owners Shipman & King acquired it in 1976.

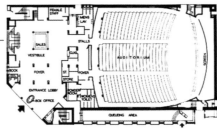
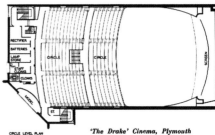

'The Drake' Cinema, Plymouth

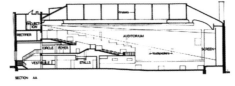

Top: *The ABC Cinema, the Athenaeum and the Drake in 1970.*
Middle: *Plans of the Drake pre-conversion to triple screen.*
Bottom: *Douglas Mounce interviews Morecombe and Wise — 'Get our of that!'.*

Top: *Pictures of Emerson Lake and Palmer's debut gig in the Guildhall, on 23 August 1970, taken by Tony Byers who trained on local papers in Plymouth before joining BBC South West. Greg Van Dike's band Earth supported ELP at the gig and very nearly got signed that day. The band included Greg, Pete Spearing and Ian Snow and it soon after evolved into Stonehouse, who were signed by RCA. Middle left to right: Hawkwind, Stray at the Van Dike, Jethro Tull (Guildhall) and Pink Floyd (Van Dike). Bottom: David Bowie at the Guildhall, tickets, 60p. Manfred Mann's Earthband a the Guildhall, and Rennaisance at the Van Dike — note the giant Beardsley prints on each side of the stage.*

The explosion of British popular music in the early Sixties had led to a massive boom in musical genres. By the beginning of the Seventies, we had pop, rock, psychedelic rock, progressive rock, folk rock, jazz rock, blues, reggae, soul, rhythm and blues ... as well as the more traditional strands of jazz and folk and mainstream music.

As the Seventies evolved we had pomp rock, glam rock, punk rock, pub rock, rock steady, ska, and 'new wave'.

Furthermore each style tended to attract its own niche audiences, so it became increasingly common for venues to associate themselves with more than just a few of these categories.

Clearly a few managed it, especially the larger venues, like the ABC (until the mid-Seventies) and the Guildhall, as it wasn't viable to stage the bigger acts in some of the City's smaller venues.

What happened in practice, though, was that a handful of venues quickly built a reputation for presenting artists and bands that were 'cool' within their field and so punters would often go along trusting that the promoter had booked something that justified the ticket price.

Foremost among those local promoters were Peter Van Dike and his son Greg. Peter was a musician-cum-photographer who had met and married singer and actress June Marlow when they were both with Eddie Mendoza's comedy dance band.

Peter set up the Van Dike Club in a social club in Exmouth Road, Devonort, in the late-Sixties and it quickly became one of the most celebrated venues on the slightly alternative circuit. Free, Family, Fleetwood Mac, Fairport Convention, Jethro Tull, Genesis, Pink Floyd, Tyrannosaurus Rex, Matthews Southern Comfort, Status Quo, Traffic, Yes, David Bowie, Cat Stevens, Eric Clapton (in his Derek and the Dominoes mode) all played the venue, along with dozens of other bands, until the police, who were stationed across the road from the venue, became overly suspicious about some of the substances that some of the concert-goers were consuming.

Van Dike continued promoting bands however, and the Guildhall was, for a time, the venue of choice. Here Roxy Music made an early appearance, as well as Wizzard, Elton John, ELO, Focus and many others, most notably Emerson, Lake and Palmer, the so-called supergroup, who played their first ever gig in Plymouth just a week or so before performing at the 1970 Isle of Wight Festival.

Greg Van Dike later recalled that Messrs Emerson, Lake and Palmer had all played the Van Dike club in their previous bands (Nice, King Crimson and Atomic Rooster respectively). They had got on well with Peter and were looking to do a low-key gig ahead of the big festival. Greg subsequently revived the Exmouth Road premises as the Metro, featuring a mix of live bands and Greg's Video-Disco.

By this stage the scene had moved on a little and bands included Magazine, the Rezillos, Ultravox, Ian Dury and The Jam (who appeared at the Fiesta Suite).

Above: Interior and exterior views of the Van Dike Club in Exmouth Road.

One great gig at the end of the Seventies, at the Fiesta Suite, saw the 2 Tone Tour of 1979 featuring Madness, Specials and The Selecter. The place was jumping, literally, so much so that the restaurateur below the venue went up to complain that he thought his ceiling was going to come down. Another night saw Iron Maiden play an early gig at the Fiesta, while Blondie and the Ramones played at the Top Rank Suite.

By this time, however, there was another venue that was becoming a major draw in town for a certain section of the music following population — Woods. It operated out of the erstwhile Park Ballroom, above Burton's tailors, at the top of Old Town Street, on the corner with Eastlake Street.

With a much edgier feel this was where some of the better-known punk and new-wave artists played, their names redolent of the angry reaction to the fact that the bands that were ruling the roost up until this point were largely well-established 'dinosaurs' of rock. The feeling was that it was time for the young generation to make their own music again. And so came the Furious Pigs, the Slits, Slack Alice, the Saints and the Sex Pistols.

The most notorious of them all, the Sex Pistols, played Woods twice, once on their Anarchy tour, and once, after they'd been banned from most towns and cities as SPOT (or the Sex Pistols On Tour – for those in the know).

I managed to get a lengthy interview with them at the time. They were staying in the Holiday Inn. They giggled, belched, farted and swore their way through the 40-minute audience I was granted with them. They knew nothing about anarchy, but I was able to use some of the material for a thesis I was writing then about youth culture. Sadly the tape was stolen a few years later, along with a batch of other tapes. A pity, as it was priceless in more ways than one!

The band swore on stage too, although they made no attempt to incite the trouble they spoke of. It was an interesting era. Spitting was another punk phenomenon. When The Damned played Castaways, on Union Street, ,one of the fans spat at the bass player, who promptly thrust his guitar at the hapless punter's forehead and knocked him unconscious!

Swearing on stage was considered shocking rather than commonplace in the Seventies and while the punk groups were out to shock, down the road at the Friary Folk Club, life was altogether more civilised, even if some of the acts might have had a genuinely more political agenda. Bill Long was the promoter there: *'We started out at the Friary pub at Bretonside. Every Sunday night at 8pm: Jasper Carrott played there on 8 August 1971, the week after Decameron and the week before Derek Brimstone.*

Promotional material for various venues and gigs.

'Jasper was the best remembered of them all, and each time we had him back we'd have to get a bigger venue. I think we had him later that year at the Lower Guildhall, then the New Continental, the Fiesta Suite in Mayflower Street, and, just before Christmas 1974, the Rainbow Room of the Good Companions.

'Another real star we had down was the French fiddle player, Stephan Grapelli – it was an honour to work with him. The Westward TV anchorman, Stuart Hutchinson, acted as master of ceremonies that evening for nothing. I hid away – but they made sure I got the credit for the gig.

'Another time we had Jake Thackeray, who wrote those very dry, witty songs (notably on Braden's Week and then That's Life with Esther Ranzen), but was famous for never really smiling himself. However when I was taking a glass of water up to him, I slipped and fell and he laughed like anything, I had to laugh too.'

But even the cosy folk world had its moments, as Bill recalls: 'It wasn't so funny when we had Don Partridge here. He had a couple of big hits with his quirky one-man-band songs and the Lord Mayor came to see his gig. Don hadn't quite adjusted to his new-found status and actually thought it was clever to insult the Lord Mayor. It was very embarrassing – I wrote a letter of apology to the Lord Mayor afterwards.'

The leading lights of the folk scene in Plymouth in the late Seventies were the four-piece Dockyard and Warships. They were residents at the Navy Inn Folk Club on the Barbican for 10 years — one of the best folk clubs in the UK. The band played clubs and festivals and were often on the radio, as well as, occasionally, on local TV. Guitarist Graham Lobb presented a folk programme on Plymouth Sound too.

And why the band name? Geoff Lakeman explained: 'Joy and I arrived in the City as a duo and met Graham and Val who had previously run folk clubs with people like Cyril Tawney. They were asked to do a big concert at the Guildhall as a support for Maddy Pryor (of Steeleye Span) but didn't fancy doing it as a duo. They asked us to form an instant quartet and we didn't know what to call ourselves. Val — who worked at a Lloyds Bank in the City- — was walking on the Hoe during a lunch break, heard the boat-trip hawker yelling " Dockyards and Warships, Dockyards and Warships!"

'And that was it. We thought the name personified everything about Plymouth as a seaside city. Trouble is every time we did a gig up-country people were expecting a bunch of hairy-assed shanty singers to arrive.'

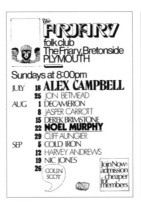

A selection of Roy Perring's fine folk club posters and a photo of Dockyard and Warships taken at the BBC Spotlight studios during a live programme. L to R. Joy Lakeman on fiddle, Geoff on concertina, Val Lobb on vocals (and whistle) and Graham Lobb on guitar.

As well as visiting groups and artists, Plymouth had a vibrant music scene of its own. In addition to venues like the aforementioned Woods, Van Dike Club, Fiesta Suite, Continental Hotel, and the Guildhall, there was the Top Rank Suite, the Polytechnic Main Hall and a host of pubs promoting live music. Notable among the pubs were the Breakwater at Cattedown; the Ark Royal, the Old Chapel, the Swan at Devonport, the Cherry Tree at Pennycross and the Good Companions in town.

Local folkies included Porrij, the Pheasant Pluckers, and Jon Benns. Rockier material came courtesy of bands like Asgaerd, Badger, Commune, Quarry, Hombre, Stonehouse and Spare Parts. Towards the end of the decade a few younger outfits popped up: Kid Cairo and the Nation, the Catholics, Monster Gut and the pleasantly punky-cum-rocksteady ensemble, the Bricks.

Stonehouse were Pete Spearing, Jimmy Smith, Ian Snow and Terry Parker. In 1971 they released a self-penned album, Stonehouse Creek, that was steeped in the music of that era — Free, Deep Purple and Led Zeppelin.

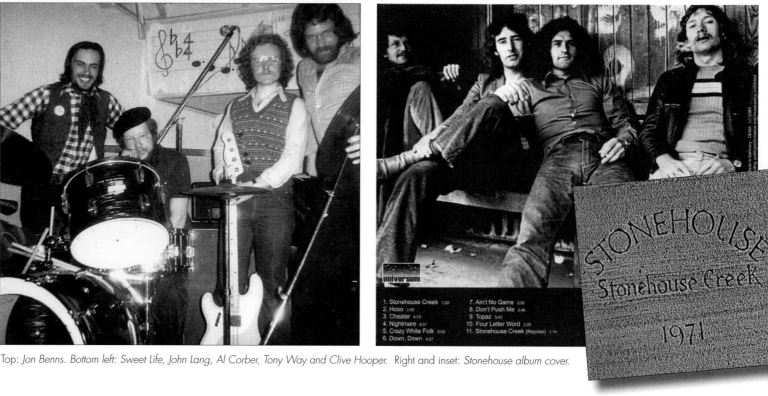

Top: Jon Benns. Bottom left: Sweet Life, John Lang, Al Corber, Tony Way and Clive Hooper. Right and inset: Stonehouse album cover.

Top: *Hombre abroad, in 1978, Clive Hooper, Russ Aisthorpe, Tony Way, Doc Meen, Mike Pawley.* Middle: *The Bricks, who were Paul MacDougall, Viva Hammell, Kevin Ward, Helen Ham, Al Sperring, Andy Martin, Ric Gadsby.* Bottom: *Helen and Viva.* Top right: *The Catholics with Nick Sims.* Bottom: *Monster Gut, with Dave Behennah, roaming Peverell's back lanes.*

For those not into the 'in scene', there was plenty of other music on offer. Plymouth has never been short of musicians who have cut their teeth with Royal Marine bands over the years. Russ Thomas was one of the more conspicuous former bandsmen on the local circuit in the Seventies. Originally from Wales, Russ had played with Harry Pook for sometime before forming his own Showband to take over from Les Watts, who had been the resident function band at the Duke of Cornwall.

In a similar vein, Chris Costin, ex-Royal Navy and Sutton High School, was another former Harry Pook man, and he formed his Magic Showband in the late-Sixties. They played dinner-dances, balls and functions throughout the decade.

Gordon Clarke was another familiar figure on the circuit, his drums lending a backbeat to many combos over the years, including, for a spell with the Angela Christian Trio. Gordon also played with Les Watts, the Banjo Bone Band and fellow local jazz men Mike Westbrook and John Surman, both highly respected recording artists, as indeed was another Plymouth-born jazz hero, Rod Mason.

Rod had joined the Cy-Laurie band back in the Fifties as a nineteen-year-old. In 1962 he teamed up with Monty Sunshine and then in 1970 became a star part of Acker Bilk's Paramount Jazz Band. In 1973 he formed a new band with Ian Wheeler and went on to cut a great many recordings, including the 1977 set 'Good Companions', recorded in London with Johnny Withers on banjo, Chris Haskins on bass, Pete Allen, on sax and clarinet, and Jimmy Garforth on drums. The Millbridge in Stoke, the Bird Cage Club, the Safari Club in Notte Street, and the Plymouth Constitutional Club in Elliot Street on the Hoe, were among the regular haunts for jazzers.

Not so local, but always pulling a good crowd, was Ivy Benson's band. Formed during the Second World War and featuring an estimated 250 female musicians over the years — it was an all-girl band — the line-up at one time included local lass Sheila Tracy on trombone. In later years she moved into television and was a regular on the BBC's local evening news programme Spotlight.

In 1974 Sheila made the news herself when she became the first female newsreader on BBC Radio 4.

Top: *The Magic Showband: Dave White, Fraser Weeks, Barry Poppy, Chris, Alan Collins, Tony Evans, Ian, anon, Dave Brimble. Middle: Russ Thomas band — Colin Bath, Tony Mitchell, Robin (Red Barron) Bowles, Bern Stewart, Eric Pearn, Russ, John Bushel, Carl Joliffe, Dave McCracken, Steve Smith. Bottom: Angela Christian Trio with Gordon Clarke on drums.*

Top: *The Ivy Benson Band.* Right: *The Banjo Bone Band.* Left: *Rod Mason's Jass Band on the Hoe.*
Inset: *Cover of Rod's Good Companions album.*

RECORD SHOP

SHOP

RECORD SHOP

NEVER MIND THE BOLLOCKS HERE'S THE SEX PISTOLS

There was barely a band or artist that didn't aspire to produce a record in the Seventies. Sales of vinyl reached an all-time high midway through the decade. Indeed it has been said that for a while the music business was even bigger than Hollywood.

Hundreds of millions of discs were manufactured and sold every year — it was truly the golden age of the 12-inch 33.33 revolutions per minute album … and sales of the 7-inch 45 rpm single were almost as impressive.

It helped that there were plenty of outlets to buy them from: WH Smiths, Arcadia, the Co-op, City Radio, Dingles, Boots, Moons, Woolworths, Littlewoods and others all had record departments and then there were the specialists like Peter Russell's wonderful, jazz-flavoured, Hot Record Store and the fledgling Virgin Records, each of them situated near an entrance of the Pannier Market.

Most of them had listening booths: some were like padded, windowless phone boxes where you could stand and listen before making a purchase; others were more like a space where you placed your head between speakers in a kind of mini head-only booth, to get the full effect of the stereo, or yet others, towards the end of the decade, had headphones you could wear.

With very few album tracks being aired on either Radio 1 or Radio 2, and little other choice of listening available, they fulfilled a very useful purpose, as did reviews in the popular music press, dominated by Sounds, the New Musical Express and Melody Maker.

Opposite page: Dingles record department with a few of the decades best sellers. Top left: The Fiesta DJ. Top right: DJ Andy Howard, aka Andy Razor, makes his debut in Woods. Middle: Pete Russell's Hot Record Store, Frankfort Gate.

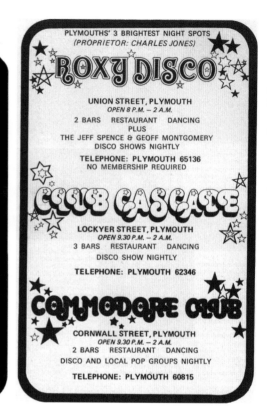

If record sales peaked in the Seventies, so too did their use as means of entertaining people, as this was also the golden age of the discotheque.

The young generation had been dancing to discs, spun by Disc Jockeys, since the mid-Sixties. The Top Rank Ballroom in Union Street had been one of the first, locally, to embrace the new phenomenon, with Mike Turner and Robert Catterall (Bobby Cee) among the first generation of local DJs. Bobby Cee regularly wore a DJ too, as in dinner jacket. Certainly in the early days a dress code applied on the dance floor at the Majestic, you'd be lucky to get in without a tie. By the Seventies regulations had been relaxed, as the Top Rank Organisation themselves were keen to point out:

'Suddenly, everything's changed. And it's all happening at Top Rank. New bands, new atmosphere, great vibes. So come as you like, wear what you like, and dance what you like.'

By that stage, of course, the Rank Organisation had a lot more competition. Plymouth's teenagers and party people now had a bewildering range of venues to choose from. Club owners spent ever-increasing amounts attempting to entice people their way.

The students and the rockier, generally hairier, set were attracted to Chris Redding at Woods, Andy Howard's Rock Show, Benny's 'Eavy Metal Disco and the Ark Roadshow in the Lower Guildhall. Ronnie's on the Barbican, Tramps at Bretonside, Pinkies on Mutley Plain and the OPM Club in Efford, were on the list with a few more besides.

The main money, though, was spent on and at the Fiesta Suite in Mayflower Street, Tiffs in Town in Union Street, and the three clubs run by Charles Jones — the Roxy Disco in Union Street, Club Cascade in Lockyer Street, and the Commodore Club in Cornwall Street — all of them with their own restaurant facility.

For the slightly more adventurous there was also Mr Harry's on the Hoe and Diamond Lil's, with Ronnie Potter, in Union Street.

Such was the popularity of the disco however, that many DJs took their shows on the road, Peter Greig, Peter Gunn, Gary Lyons, Jeff Spence and Ian Calvert among them. The mobile jocks were particularly popular with the out-of-town venues, like the Falstaff at Southway, the Glen at Glenholt, the Lion and Column at Ham, the Tiger at Whitleigh, and the Mountbatten at Hooe, where Peter Greig's Route 66 disco was almost a fixture.

These places also supported an element of live music in what was a very vibrant night life in the city.

Opposite page: *Posters and adverts.* Top left: *Chinese New Year dragon at the Top Rank Suite.* Middle: *A hen night at the Majestic — Jackie Milford, Linda Moon (soon to be Moulder), club bouncer, June Northcott, Sue Kemp, Helen Stroud. Front; Julie Walsh and June Howells.* Bottom: *Inside the Fiesta.* Above: *Exterior view.*

Social clubs — Civil Service, Armed Services, British Legion, etc — and the bigger hotels were also regularly in the market for booking entertainment of one form or another. In the early Seventies especially, the Continental Hotel looked to do something quite unusual locally — book a show for the whole summer.

Generally competing with a Hoe Theatre Summer Show, the Continental had the advantage of being more handy for their guests and for those of the Duke of Cornwall across the road, although it's debatable as to how keen they would have been to promote it.

Advertising itself as *'Music Hall Variety Show with full professional cast'*. Local man Johnny Billington hosted the 1972 extravaganza which included Alana *'our vivacious soubrette from London, who has sung and danced her way around the world'*, Danni Danion, *'a handsome Parisian who sings in no less than nine languages'*, a couple of dancers and musicians and Douglas Mounce — *'a young man with great zest and a slick sense of humour'*.

There were, of course, a whole stack of other artists who were 'entertainers' on the circuit, among them the Georgia Boys, a duo formed by Pete Martin, who did voice-overs for all the American-sounding adverts on Plymouth Sound and drove a big American car.

Top: *The Continental Hotel*. Above: *Introductory programme*. Right: *Georgia Boys promo material*.

Other notable venues around town included Plymouth Arts Centre, which staged small-scale theatrical productions — Foots Barn, founded in 1971, were regulars — as well as music, film and, of course, art. In the mid-Seventies Arts Centre Director, Bernard Samuels, was tipped off about the work of a fifty-year-old woman who ran a guest house on the Hoe and in November 1975 he staged the first ever exhibition of Beryl Cook's work in Looe Street.

The exhibition was an instant success and attracted interest from the national media, the *Sunday Times* put her 1974 painting of a scene from the Lockyer Tavern on the cover of their colour supplement.

In 1978 her first book was published. The following year she appeared on the South Bank Show, where she talked about her work to the show's host Melvyn Bragg.

Before long Beryl became one of the best-known people associated with the City, along with the likes of Saltash-born concert pianist Moura Lympany and Plymouth-born composer and conductor Ron Goodwin, whose output included *633 Squadron* and *Force Ten From Navarone*, partly filmed in Devonport Dockyard's South Yard.

Clockwise from top: *Royal Ballet in Central Park: the Sunday Times feature that told the world about Beryl Cook; Ron Goodwin and Moura Lympany.*

Plymouth's principal theatre throughout the Seventies though, was the Hoe Theatre. It was still relatively new then, having opened as a 600-seater, prefabricated, wooden, single-storey, somewhat draughty affair, in 1962. Replacing the earlier Hoe Summer Marquee, the building was re-roofed and renovated in the Seventies. Much was done to broaden its appeal and its offer.

As well as the annual summer shows, pantomimes and locally produced plays became part of the Hoe's staple fare.

Impressario John Redgrave's pantomimes proved particularly popular. Indeed Herald critic Harvey Crane described his 1976 production of *Cinderella* as *'the best panto seen for a long time, and by far the best and most outstanding amongst the other South West shows.'* Clearly Redgrave's success gave him food for thought and two years later he bought and restored the Palace Theatre. He opened his 1978 panto, a revival of his *Cinderella* show with Frankie Howerd, Julian Orchard, Peter Jones, John Boulter and Shuni Starr as Cinders.

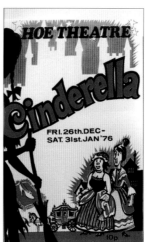

This page: *These programmes demonstrate the wide variety of shows that were on offer at the Hoe Theatre throughout the Seventies.*

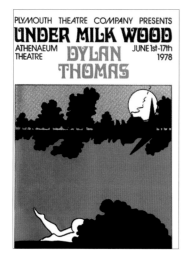

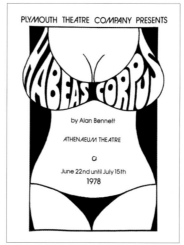

In 1972, following on from the Theatre for Plymouth Company, the Plymouth Theatre Company was formed. The Artistic Director was the 30-year-old Canadian Bob Hamlin and under his command the Company staged five or six productions a year, some at the Hoe and some at the Athenaeum Theatre.

The .Athenaeum had opened the year before the Hoe and neither were particularly well-regarded in theatrical circles. Indeed, in his book the *Playbill: A History of Theatre in the West Country*, Harvey Crane went further by suggesting that *'Plymouth's half-hearted attempts over the years since the Second World War to build a theatre made the city into something of a laughing stock in the theatre world.*

'This refusal to take theatre seriously was evidenced by some Plymouth councillors who seemed to regard drama as frivolous and not falling into the category of higher things such as education, libraries, art galleries, swimming pools, shops, drains and roads or civic dignity.'

Harvey did however concede that the plans announced in the late-Seventies to build a decent theatre in Plymouth had *'just about redeemed the city's reputation'.*

This page: A few Athenaeum programmes, including the 1979 romp *Bedroom Farce* that starred *Hugh Paddick, Nyree Dawn Porter, Tim Brook-Taylor and Leslie Phillips.*

This page: Palace productions ranged from elaborate amateur shows and extravagant pantos to manic puppets and pajama-less nakedness.

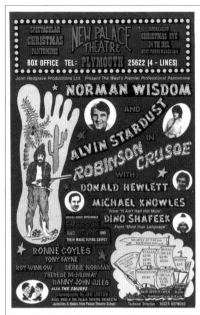

The decision to construct a grand new theatre at the top end of Union Street was undoubtedly a cause for concern for John Redgrave, however, as he had just invested in the revival of the Palace Theatre. Would there a big enough audience for both?

Certainly it wasn't an easy ride for the Palace and in a bid to stay viable they tried everything there – pantomime, pop, drama and variety.

Local amateur company the Carmenians staged some lavish productions there including a special Jubilee Year version of Showboat. Other visitors to the Palace included Rod Hull and Emu, Paul Raymond Pin Up, and star of such Seventies cinematic 'classics' as *Exposé*, *Hardcore* and *Let's Get Laid* — Fiona Richmond — who appeared in *Yes We Have No Pajamas*.

Meanwhile, largely hidden away in the Royal Marine Barracks at Stonehouse, was another lovely little theatre that staged only occasional, but very welcome, productions — the Globe. It was the oldest of all the local playhouses. The cosy 252-seater venue was opened in 1820 in a disused racquets court.

Top: Pantos were particularly popular at the Palace, the Christmas 1979 production of Robinson Crusoe with Norman Wisdom and Alvin Stardust ran through to 15 March the following year. Photo shows Norman with a young Beverley Kinsella. Above: Palace in 1977 with Carmenians' Showboat.

Having opened on Thursday 19 April 1962 at a cost of £30,000, Plymouth Zoo sadly closed its doors for the final time on Sunday 8 January 1978.

Open for barely 16 years, the zoo had provided a lot of entertainment and interest over its comparatively short stay in Central Park, like the time that Snowy the deer went for a jaunt around Milehouse one morning after someone had left the back gate of the zoo open overnight.

Zoo manager George Hughton and his staff caught up with Snowy in Segrave Road. She eluded her would-be captors though and later collided with a moving car crossing back over Outland Road.

A crowd of about 100 later watched her munching leaves near the tennis courts by Central Park pool and eventually she was recaptured with the help of a goal net from Argyle.

A skateboard park was created on the site soon after the zoo closed.

Top: *Young Derek Tait at Plymouth Zoo.* Bottom: *Plymouth Zoo, 1962-1978.*

Feeding the giraffes — note the Argyle floodlight pylon behind their heads.

MEDIA

At the start of the Seventies the City was served by its two long-standing daily papers, the *Western Morning News* and the *Western Evening Herald*, operating out of their pre-war offices in New George Street. Sister papers, they both cost 5d (2p), but such were the inflation rates of the decade that by 1976 both had increased their cover price by 350% to 7p. There were two other papers that covered news in the City, although to a much lesser extent — the *Sunday Independent* and it's sister paper, the *South Devon Times*, which was published every Thursday. Based in Exeter Street at the start of the decade they later moved to purpose-built premises at Burrington Way and they too experienced a massive hike in price going from 7d and 4d (3p and 2p roughly) to 12p and 8p respectively.

Other significant news providers were BBC and ITV via the magazine programmes *Spotlight South West* and *Westward Diary*.

SOUTH DEVON TIMES

5d. THURSDAY, MARCH 26, 1970 No. 2,562

Sunday Independent

The Western Morning News

WESTERN EVENING HERALD
&WESTERN EVENING NEWS

Opposite page: *Westward Television Headquarters alongside the Athenaeum.* Above: *The ABC (bottom left), Westward and the Drake Cinema, wih the Ballard Centre behind.*

At the end of April 1971 Westward Television celebrated its tenth birthday and presumably TV's most enduring, although not quite most famous, stuffed star, Gus Honeybun, waggled his ears, performed a few bunny-hops and fiddled with the studio lights. Famously Gus was better-behaved for some of the presenters than for others: for Roger Shaw he was generally very good but he could be a bit naughty for Judi Spiers and Ian Stirling.

The signature programme, *Westward Diary*, originally fronted by Barry Westwood, Reginald Bosanquet and Kenneth MacLeod, was, in the Seventies, anchored by MacLeod.

Other familiar faces included David Rodgers and Angela Rippon — who had moved across from BBC South West in 1969. Associated then with children's and women's programmes, Angela, amongst other things was, in 1972, largely responsible for producing a summer show which later laid claim to the notion that it was the first 'Open Access' show for young people in Britain. Directed by Roger Gage, the programme's team also included David Rodgers, who also had BBC connections.

In 1970, weatherman, Graham Danton was given his own stand-alone show — *A Date With Danton*. A few years later, in 1973, the Countryside Commission opened the South West Coast Path, a walk around the whole peninsula that went from Swanage in Dorest to Minehead in Somerset, via Land's End.

Top and bottom: *Behind the scenes*. Top right: *Keith Fordyce and Tony Blackburn with Miss Westward '77, Jeanette White and far right, some of the 1971 finalists*.

To recognise the fact, Westward asked one of their Diary reporters, Clive Gunnell, who had already walked and filmed the *Two Moors Walk* for the company, to walk the route and, again, film the journey. Starting out from Minehead, Clive's trek occupied several series and *Walking Westward* became one of the station's best-known programmes. Some Cornish sections of it were shown in the States as trail-blazers for the BBC's *Poldark* series when it was screened over there. Clive also fronted what was adjudged the *'Most Outstanding Regional Production of 1977'* — a film called *To Tavistock Goose Fair.* Meanwhile, other programmes produced by Westward included a number of adult-education-style outputs like the *Westcountry Fayre* cookery programme, the food-freezing series *Freeze!* and the weight conscious offering, *Keep Britain Slim.*

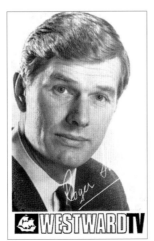

Clockwise from top left: *Stuart Hutchinson, Del Cooper, Clive Gunnell, Dorothy Innes at the Westward Studio, Ken McLeod, Ian Stirling, Roger Shaw, Judi Spiers, Graham Danton.*

David Rodgers
Morning Sou'West

Plymouth 206m Exeter 303m Torbay 351m Mid-West Cornwall 397m North Devon 439m

Meanwhile, keeping Britain tuned in, in the late-Sixties, the BBC started experimenting with local radio. Radio Leicester was the first licence to be granted in November 1968.

Others followed — Leeds, Stoke, Durham, Sheffield, Merseyside, Nottingham — but nothing further to the south and west of Brighton.

Bristol was one of several additions to the 'experiment' in 1970 and gradually more and more of the country was covered, but not the South West: — although its news had been reported for many years in local five-minute bulletins from Plymouth alongside an early 25-minute Bristol-based opt-out called *Today in the South and West* (*Tiz Waz*). The local South West radio bulletins continued through to the 80s and *Tiz Waz* was followed by a slightly longer news, current affairs, local topics and music programme going out Monday to Friday serving the region on the Radio 4 frequency called *Midday Parade*. Presented by Colm Connolly it was first aired in 1970.

That was succeeded, on 1 March 1973, by *Morning Sou' West*, a daily two-hour programme that was broadcast from the BBC's Seymour Road studios.

Chris Blount, Colin Caley, Ross Salmon, Tony Byers, David Rodgers and, pioneering female broadcaster, Peggy Archer, were among the many voices heard.

For coverage later in the day the BBC turned to regional television with four news bulletins spread across the day: lunchtime, mid-afternoon, early evening with *Spotlight*, just before *Nationwide*, and just after the *Nine O'Clock News*.

In 1968 Newcastle and Plymouth had been chosen as stations that would have the ability to fade out the national network and feed in local news and programme announcements to Devon, Cornwall, and the Channel and Scilly Island transmitters.

Angela Rippon, Joe Pengelly, and Ian Smith were chosen as the three continuity announcers who, between them, shared the rota and the responsibilities. A little later, Donald Heighway joined Joe and the team.

Meanwhile, among the other faces familiar on BBC South West during the Seventies were Hugh Scully (until 1978), Sheila Tracey (until 1973), Sue Lawley (1970-73), Kate Adie (1976), Linda Alexander (1977) and Fern Britton.

Top left: *David Rodgers, who later moved to Westward.* Right: *BBC regular anchorman Joe Pengelly.*
Bottom: *Chris Blount and Tony Byers in the Morning Sou' West studio.*

The Morning Sou' West production office in Seymour Road, with Colin Caley, Ros Carter, Ross Salmon, Guy Slatter (who moved over from Midday Parade) and Chris Blount.

213

Top: *Standing, Brian Measures, Louise Churchill, Carmella McKenzie, Peter Grieg. Seated, Ian Calvert and David Bassett.* Bottom: *Earl's Acre Studios.*

Up until 1972 the BBC had enjoyed a legal monopoly on radio broadcasting in Britain but, with the passing of The Sound Broadcasting Act that summer, it all changed.

Ever since the off-shore pirate radio stations had been shut down there had been a degree of unhappiness amongst the younger generation. Despite the creation of Radio 1, especially aimed at the young, there was a feeling that young voters had influenced the 1970 election outcome and contribution to Edward Heath's success.

Royal Acceptance of the Heath Government's bill meant that independent radio stations could now be formed along the lines of the existing ITV service and to compete with the recently established BBC Local Radio services. The Independent Television Authority (ITA) was restyled the Independent Broadcasting Authority. In 1974, Plymouth became only the ninth city in the country, outside London, to be awarded a local radio contract.

Thus it was that on Monday 19 May 1975, at six o'clock in the morning, David Bassett opened his fader and Plymouth Sound began its first ever broadcast. Cat Stevens' *Morning Has Broken* was the first disc played.

'We were the new boys in town,' recalls Malcolm Carroll, the station's main news man, not that he ever intended to be in that position.

'I had an informal, and very boozy, 'interview' with David Bassett in the Spider's Web - the downstairs bar of the Duke of Cornwall. We somehow bonded and I asked him if I'd got the job as a news reporter.'

"How would you like to be Head of News," he replied. "Why me?"

"Because I like you!" came the reply.

And that's how it was. One Friday I was working as a sub-editor on the Western Morning News, and then on the following Monday morning I was Head of News at Plymouth Sound ... and that's how Bassett always referred to me – "Head of News".

He'd greet me in the corridor and repeat his broadcasting mantra; "Ah, Head of News, smooth, tight and flowing." I'd also just stepped out of a relationship and when I remarried my wife, Su, who also came to work on the station, became "Mrs Head of News". But that was Bassett – everyone had a nickname.

'David had been in the Merchant Navy, he got into broadcasting in Canada, after he'd been taken ill and while in hospital over there somehow got involved with a radio station in Toronto. Initially I think he was on sales, but then someone at the station took ill and David was given a try out on air – he became a huge star over there.

He and Bob Hussell started Plymouth Sound. Bob had been a Fleet Street features editor and was part of a successful business family in Plymouth; he'd always dreamt of running his own station every since he was turned down for a job by the BBC. He knew David Bassett from schooldays, I think. Bob was the organised money man and David had the creative brain and the flair – but he hated paperwork – the only thing you ever saw on his desk was a small Canadian flag!

'They started the whole thing with a blank sheet of paper. We had to be different to what the BBC were doing at the time, there were tough regulations, the IBA stipulated that we had to have a significant amount of local news.

'I remember in our first week there was a bus crash on the way to Tavistock. We broke the story at 3.15, during Louise Churchill's afternoon show. Local news had never been aired so quickly before, and our phone lines were instantly jammed with calls from anxious parents.'

'Louise, of course, would later occupy a similar role to Bob, after his sad early death. She had formerly been at Westward TV in various roles.'

Other original Plymouth Sound stalwarts had also long-cherished radio ambitions, among them Australian Howard Bowles, and local DJ Ian Calvert who had almost landed a full-time Radio Luxembourg job before starting his popular evening programmes.

261 PLYMOUTH SOUND

The New One in Town –

and growing very nicely Thank-you!

261 your independent local Radio Station
on 96 VHF in stereo and Rediffusion Channel C

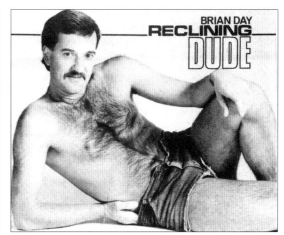

BRIAN DAY
RECLINING DUDE

Clockwise from top: Carmella McKenzie, 'Head of News' Malcolm Carroll, David Bassett, Brian Day, and Bob Hussell with a team, of presenters, workmen and station assistants, including Mike Allen, Linda Wing, John Coates (facing Bob in a 261 t-shirt), Terry Schofield

Above: *Royal Marine Band play at Home Park.* Inset: *Aerial view of Central Park, 1975.*
Opposite page: *Barn Park end is crowded, but not with away fans, for the game against Santos.*

SPORT

Plymouth Argyle started the Seventies in the Third Division of English football. Billy Bingham was the man in charge. A lack-lustre season saw them finish seventeenth, four places below Devon rivals Torquay, who also knocked them out of the League Cup.

The 1970/71 campaign was little better and, with Ellis Stuttard back at the helm, they finished fifteenth, five places below the Gulls. There was a top ten finish for Argyle in 1971/2 ... and relegation for Torquay. A poor start to the 1972 season (where they failed to score in six of their first twelve games, which included a run of five consecutive defeats) had seen a change of manager and former England international goalkeeper, 35-year-old Tony Waiters was appointed by the board.

There was a marked, but by no means radical, improvement and the team once again finished in the top ten with Neil Hague and Jimmy Hinch netting most goals and Hague winning 'Player of the Year'.

The season was remarkable for one game in particular, and it wasn't the 2-1 defeat at the hands of Leeds United at Elland Road, in the fourth round of the FA Cup in front of 38,000. It was the 3-2 win over a touring side from South America — a friendly game which attracted an equally large crowd to Home Park.

The excitement that surrounded the appearance of Brazil's finest team, Santos, on March 14 1973, was off the radar. Santos had brought with them three of Brazil's World Cup-winning squad of 1970, plus, probably the most famous footballer in the world — Pele.

Argyle were one of only two teams Santos were scheduled to play in England, the other outfit was Second Division Fulham where, two days earlier, the visitors had suffered only their second defeat in a 12-match run on the road. The crowd at Craven Cottage had been over 21,000, the biggest of their season so far, and Santos were on half of the gate money.

The tourists were not expecting such a big gate against their Third Division rivals and so agreed a figure of £2,500. However, when they got to Home Park and saw almost 40,000 squeezed in the Central Park venue, they refused to play unless they were paid another £2,500. In the interests of avoiding a riot, Argyle agreed. When club chairman Robert Daniel and secretary Graham Little handed over the money after the game, though, Daniel said: *'This is crooked, we will report you, you'll never play in this country again.'* But the Santos man simply shrugged his shoulders and said: *'Plenty more countries.'*

Clockwise from top left: *Argyle v Santos programme; Peter Darke, Colin Sullivan, Pele, Jim Furnell; Rita Daniel, Pele, and his wife Rosemeri; the Santos team; Carlos Alberto and Dave Provan lead their teams out; Pele takes the pitch.*

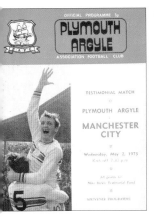
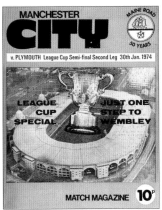

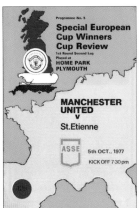

Argyle, incidentally, scored three first-half goals against Santos and at half-time Pele asked that the referee be changed. The game finished 3-2 to the Pilgrims with Pele scoring from the penalty spot.

The following season saw another undistinguished performance in the league, but great excitement in both domestic cup competitions. Having disposed of Brentford and Walsall in the first two rounds of the FA Cup, with new boy Paul Mariner scoring in both games, Argyle were drawn against Manchester United in the third round on 5 January 1974. A goal from Lou Macari was all it took to break the hearts of the many Argyle fans who swelled the ranks of the 32,000 crowd at Old Trafford.

Many of those travelling fans were back in Manchester just a few weeks later when Argyle played City in the second leg of the semi-final of the League Cup. Argyle had knocked out Torquay in the first round back in August, then Portsmouth in October, before, somewhat remarkably, claiming the scalps of three top-flight sides, Burnley, Queens Park Rangers and Birmingham City, all away from home.

In the semi-final first leg at Home Park Steve Davey found the net for the seventh time in that run of League Cup matches, which earned Argyle a draw and gave them a realistic hope of their first ever trip to Wembley as they headed for Maine Road.

However, goals from Francis Lee and Colin Bell gave City the edge. They won 2-0, although they lost the final, 1-0, to Wolves. Later in the summer they lost the Charity Shield to Burnley, whom Argyle had already beaten that season.

Curiously enough, Manchester United were relegated from the First Division that same season, but they quickly bounced back. In 1977 they beat Liverpool in the FA Cup final and a few months later — following issues around football hooliganism after their Cup Winners' Cup clash with St Etienne in France — they were forced to play their home leg in a ground at least 200km from Old Trafford. They chose Home Park, presumably, partly on the grounds that Plymouth was linked to France via the Brittany Ferry — and there aren't many English grounds that far from Manchester.

Goals from Steve Coppell and Stuart Pearson saw United win through 3-1 on aggregate. A crowd of over 31,000 witnessed the spectacle. United lost in the next round to Porto, 6-5 on aggregate. When the dust had settled on the highs and lows of the 1973/4 season there was no particular air of expectation surrounding the start of the 1974/5 campaign. After losing the first seven consecutive away games, the forecast appeared only to be for further gloom, although, in fairness, the Pilgrims were unbeaten at home.

Top: *A few Programmes from some remarkable Seventies matches.*
Right: *George Best at Home Park.*

Clockwise from top left: *Bill Pearce weighs in at the Holiday Inn, with Angela Rippon and Graham Hambly; Billy Rafferty on the charge; Mariner scores at Home Park; Peter Bridgewater, Tony Waiters, Jim Furnell, with Peter Vosper presenting an award to Brian Hall; Argyle squad 1976.*

However, after a Bury own-goal gave them their first points on the road at the end of October, everything changed.

Thereafter they enjoyed a hugely successful time on their travels, thumping Bournemouth away 7-3 and Hereford 5-1. Paul Mariner and his scoring companion Billy Rafferty were rampant and the team enjoyed a mid-season 16-match unbeaten run. Indeed going into the last match of the season the league title was in their grasp. That game was away to Peterborough, whom they had already beaten comfortably at home. What's more, the only away game they had lost since that dire start had been to Blackburn where they'd been 2-1 up at half-time (they lost 5-2). Nevertheless they couldn't get a result at London Road and ended up in second place, just one point behind Blackburn. The main thing, though, was that after seven seasons in the Third Division, Argyle were back in the second tier of English league football.

It had been a great season in the end and had even included a packed Home Park performance against Everton in the fourth round of the FA Cup. Former Arsenal apprentice, Barry Vassalo, scored in one of his rare appearances but Argyle lost

3-1. Everton went out to finalists Fulham in the next round.

Sadly, Argyle's return to Division II wasn't destined to last. Failing to win a single away game in the whole of the 1975/6 season, they finished 16th, thanks to a reasonably strong set of showings at Home Park.

The following season started brightly enough. Paul Mariner scored in each of the first five games, but his sparring partner, Billy Rafferty, had already been sold and at the end of September Mariner too was on his way — to Ipswich.

The deal, worth £220,000, was the biggest to date for both clubs. Argyle received £175,000 cash, plus Terry Austin and John Peddelty.

But the real talent had gone and with it Argyle's tenuous grip on Division II football. Argyle spent the rest of the decade languishing in Division III under a variety of managers: Mike Kelly, Lennie Lawrence, Bobby Saxton, and Malcolm Allison. Relegated in 1977, and losing to lower-league Exeter, at home and away, in the League Cup, they finished just a few points short of the drop, and further ignominy, in 1978 and 1979.

Top: New strip — Keith Blunt, Nigel Menhenick, Paul Barron, Doug Collins, Neil Ramsbottom, Tony Waiters and Brian Hall. Above: Argyle announcing team — Doug Mounce, Chris Wood, Chris and Des Robinon.

Above, left to right: Fred Binney; former Tamar Schoolboy, George Foster (It was in 1977 that I started producing player cartoons for Gordon Ward in the Far Post Club); Paul Mariner and Billy Rafferty celebrate promotion.

Clockwise from top left: *September 1971, crowd at the Albion v London Welsh game; OPM Rugby squad 1971-72 — Alan Harris, Chris Banbury, Phil Jones, Jim Swales, John Perry, Nigel Byrne, Martin O'Gara, Ian Punchard, Kingsley Bishop, Peter Organ. Seated, Ian Smith, Mike Griffiths, Roger Reid, Doug Martin, Nick Partridge, Andrew Ashley, and Dave Elliott; Nick Vosper picks up Seven's Trophy, with Roger Jewell, Geoff Fabian and Malcolm Shillabeer; February 1971, Albion players clap Newton Abbot off the pirch.*

Rugby, locally, still revolved around friendlies and cup competitions, most notably the long-standing Lockie Cup, which had been contested by teams of the Three Towns and District since at least the beginning of the twentieth century.

Both Albion and the Royal Naval Engineering College teams celebrated their centenaries in the Seventies, while the OPMs celebrated their half-century. Albion were based at Beacon Park, RNEC at Manadon and OPMs at Efford.

Argaum came close to buying their own ground, with support from the Rugby Football Union, but a change of heart by the vendor at the last minute scuppered the deal.

Barry Rees, Frank Lavis, Dave Sharpe, Peter Green, F Rogers, Geoff Baskerville, Steve Body, and Huywell Phillips were the skippers that saw them through the decade.

Plymouth Albion, though, were the biggest rugby club in the area, indeed they were probably the best west of Bath and one of the top 30 clubs in the country.

And still, across the Rugby Union generally, there was no question of the sort of financial remuneration that was already in danger of crippling some of the Association Football clubs in England, from a player and from a fan's perspective.

However, as part of their centenary celebrations, Albion did splash out on one major investment — floodlights.

DHS Old Boy, and an occasional Albion hooker in the late Seventies, Charles Evans, recalls being back from Liverpool University when the first ever floodlit game was played in Plymouth:

'It was in 1976 and we played London Welsh at Beacon Park. They were one of the top sides in the country and were on their way home from a tour of Canada. They had former Welsh International, John Taylor, in their side.

'More than 3,000 people turned out to watch, Albion rarely, if ever, attracted that sort of number. Nick Vosper was Albion's star player at the time, Gary Lovell and Les Ware were other key players for Albion.'

The arrival of Marjons in Plymouth also helped to swell the Albion ranks, as players like Ian Perkins, Simon Jones, and Nigel Sparrow ended up playing at Beacon Park, along with one or two ALbion juniors, like Terry Chapman and Chris Hocking, who went into the senior pack.

From the top: *RNEC Manadon v DHSOB, at Manadon, January 1972; Navy Cup match at Keyham, 1976; March 1972 RNEC, in their centenary year, play BRNC.*

223

Clockwise from top left: *August 1971, Co-op Bowls at Unity Park; 1972 new Civil Service clubhouse and entrance underway at Beacon Park; Ladies bowls on the Hoe, c.1973; opening of the 1971 season for the Sir Francis Drake Bowling Club.*

In other sports, the Plymouth Civil Service Sports and Leisure Club saw a series of major improvements to its facilities.

In 1970 work there began on a new clubhouse which was finally completed a few years later after an investment of some £62,000.

The official opening was on 8 October 1973 and the Chairman of the Civil Service Social Club, Sir Louis Petch, was on hand to perform the official duties with Lady Petch.

An instant success, the new facility attracted greater numbers than anticipated and the membership soon soared to 15,000.

The improvements didn't stop there though and in 1975 another £20,000 of work was done to the playing fields and bowling greens.

With numbers still buoyant, turnover in their 50th anniversary year, 1977, topped an impressive £300,000 and further spending was agreed: it included new tennis courts and an extension to the social hall kitchen.

Before the decade was out the CSSC had agreed to build a new sports hall and overhaul the grounds for an even more substantial investment figure — £451,000.

Elsewhere, the OPM Club at Efford doubled the size of their sports' social facility, one of the few late-night drinking venues in the city.

There were improvements too at Home Park, where following the arrival of Bill Pearce, as Argyle's commercial manager in 1972, the financial position had improved significantly. Indeed so successful was the Argyle lottery set up by Bill that club officials from all over the country were coming to Plymouth to see what he was doing.

Another of his initiatives was to purchase a portabcabin that he'd seen in the grounds of Exeter's newest hospital and have it transferred to Home Park. Secured with the help of a loan from Watney's, the Far Post Club, as Bill christened it, was gutted and refitted and, in 1975, formally opened by Liverpool legend Bill Shankly.

Such was its popularity that within two years Watneys had been re-imbursed and the club had become a Free House. Gordon Ward was appointed bar manager. I was soon afterwards commissioned to produce a series of player cartoons to decorate the pelmet-boarding above the bar.

Meanwhile, in 1974, promising plans were announced for a new £80,000 sports complex at Peverell, with provision for two more squash courts, a kitchen, bar, lavatories, and a hall suitable for indoor football, hockey, tennis, badminton, volleyball, and basketball.

There was also the major new Mayflower Sports Hall across from Home Park, which had opened at the beginning of the decade.

Top: *Hockey at Manadon 1976.* Bottom: *OPM Hockey 2nd XI 1971-72 Bob Pratt (umpire), Pete Heath, Steve Welsh, Keith Pring, Mike Scott, David Willis, Harry Roskruge, kneeling, Andy Viner, Bryan Johnson, Pat Newnham, John Leonard, David Viner.*

Local girl, Jeanette Simpson, was there handling the Press Relations: *'Poor Bill Simpson lost his front teeth, the ball went into his face, but fortunately I used to be a dental nurse on Mutley Plain in the Fifties and I was able to get him fixed up with a temporary set quite quickly.'*

As for the game, the home side posted a score of 257 and the Taverners were slipping behind until local schoolmaster and cricket coach John Stevens came to bowl at Barrington. John subsequently said he wasn't

Plymouth Cricket Club was based at Peverell. Their art deco, two-storey clubhouse hosting a number of famous names, thanks principally to a few celebrity-style events, like the 'single wicket' tournament that took place there in the summer of 1970.

The tournament was a fund-raiser for Devon County Youth Association and was largely organised by local BBC man Ross Salmon who was a one-time colleague of Brian Johnston and John Arlott on the Test Match commentary team, as well as being a former trialist with Middlesex CC and Chelsea FC.

Those taking part included England stars; John Edrich, John Snow, Basil D'Oliveira and Freddie Trueman; as well as visiting West Indians; Lance Gibbs, Rohan Kanhai and Clive Lloyd. John Pearn was one of three local schoolboys given the honour of playing, while Peter Isbell and Martin Baxter were among the lads who made up the fielding sides. Pearn reached the semi-final before being knocked out by John Edrich who, in turn, lost the final to Northamptonshire's Hylton Ackerman.

The following season, a Lord's Taverners side were in the city to play a United Services Mayflower XI, at Mount Wise, as a fund-raiser for the National Playing Fields Association.

Fern Britton's father, actor Tony Britton, was in the line-up while other stars playing that day included John Alderton (*Please Sir*), Tim Brooke-Taylor (pre-*Goodies*), Bill Crozier, Bernard Cribbins, and Bill Simpson (*Dr Finlay's Casebook*), while the recently retired Ken Barrington was among the professional cricketers on parade.

interested in taking wickets: *'I just wanted to see these men at their best. It was a charity match and certainly the audience hadn't come to see me bowl, they wanted to see him bat. It gave me immense pleasure that I could put the ball near enough where he wanted it and see him send it sailing over the Mount Wise pavilion.'*

Barrington was on about 85 when John started to bowl, he finished on 114 and Taverners won off the penultimate ball of the game.

Meanwhile, one Plymouth star who made a bit of a name for himself in the Seventies was local darts player Cliff 'Ticker' Inglis. In 1974, aged 39, Cliff won the inaugural Phonogram World Masters Darts competition and the following year was a Unicorn World Darts Championship finalist. He finished runner-up in the Indoor Darts league, screened by Yorkshire Television.

Then in 1975 he got himself into the Guinness Book of World Records for a stunning performance, winning a 1001 game, in a Devon working men's club, in just 19 throws, his scores — 160, 180, 140, 180, 121, 180, 40.

Opposite page: Cricket at Mount Wise. Inset: *The 1970 Taverners line up at Mount Wise; Bill Crozier, Bill Simpson and Jeanette Simpson. Top left: John Edrich, Peter Isbell and Martin Baxter lead the players off the pitch at Peverell. Top right: John Stevens, with tie, West Indian Clive Lloyd and Somerset's Peter Robinson walk out to the middle, Freddie Trueman is in the doorway. Right: Cliff "Ticker" Inglis, from the Longroom pub, Stonehouse, wins the first ever World Masters Darts Championship*

Cycling was one of those growing sports in the Seventies and the staging of the start of the 1973 Milk Race in the City undoubtedly gave bicycling a big boost locally.

The Milk Marketing Board had started sponsoring the event — a sort of British equivalent of the Tour de France — in 1958, although the race had existed, in one form or another, since just after the war in 1945, when it ran from Brighton to Glasgow.

In 1973 the gruelling 1730-mile road race went from Plymouth to Paignton and in a dozen subsequent stages called at Cardiff, Aberystwyth, Kidderminster, Stoke, Leicester, Sheffield, Harrogate, Scarborough, Durham and Penrith before concluding in Blackpool.

That same year crash-helmets became compulsory for all British Cycling Federation road events, as well as for closed-circuit and track racing — itself an indication of how widespread cycling was becoming and an acknowledgement of how, with more traffic than ever before on the road, the wearing of cycle safety-helmets was to be encouraged generally.

There was a further fillip to the domestic success of cycling in 1973, when one of the sport's great British heroes, 33-year-old Barry Hoban, who had competed in the 1960 summer Olympics, became the first Briton to win two stages of the Tour de France.

Opposite page: *It's Plymouth's Hire A Bike week, a promotion outside the Council House,* in 1975. Above right: Scenes from Plymouth's International Cycling Week in 1975.
Above left: *Plymouth College Inter-City Cycle Marathon cycling team with Michael Moore, Roger Punch and Geoff Fulford.*

Having previously won single stages of the race four times in the Sixties, few would have ever anticipated that he would get to compete in a Tour de France in the Seventies starting in England.

The race had been going since 1903 and had never been off the Continent.

But in 1973 the Plymouth to Roscoff ferry link had come into service and, more significantly perhaps, Britain had joined the Common Market. That same year a party of our leading local figures, including the leader of the City Council, Alderman Harold Pattinson and the Lord Mayor, Jack Luce, had visited their counterparts in Brest – its twin town since 1963, when Harold had been Lord Mayor.

During that 1973 visit their host, Brest's Mayor, Monsieur Georges Lombard, announced that Brest had succeeded in securing the prestigious start of the 1974 Tour de France race and asked if Plymouth might agree to hosting one of the stages of the event.

On their return, despite their lack of experience in such matters, the council voted to put aside £40,000 to meet the costs involved.

Clearly there were to be a lot of issues, first among them, where to send the cyclists and how to ensure that the roads chosen could be closed. The road around Burrator Reservoir was an option, but was quickly ruled out on the grounds that it was too narrow and too short. Dartmoor was considered but thought to be impractical on the grounds it would be hard to stop animals straying on to the course. In the event, a section of the newly opened (1971) Plympton Bypass was chosen – the stretch between Marsh Mills and the Deep Lane junction. The distance between the two points is a little under four miles and offered the cyclists a circuit of 7.5 miles, which they would have to complete 14 times to measure up to the required total for a full stage of the race.

The logistics of closing this busy road in both directions for however long (each lap took approximately 15 minutes) were obviously enormous, and the implications for tourists towing caravans and all the other holiday traffic – it was to be staged on the last Friday in June – were immense.

Then there was the question of where to site vantage points for the anticipated 75,000 spectators that were predicted to want to witness this world famous event coming to mainland Britain for the first time.

As it transpired the organisation was hailed as a great success – the only major criticism falling on the shoulders of the Exeter airport

customs officials who created an inordinately long delay as they vetted the 124 riders coming in and out of the country, leaving them all with little enthusiasm to repeat the English experiment.

Television coverage also turned out to be disappointing and although the publicity was good and the backing from the local press was excellent, only an estimated 15,000 turned out to cheer on the participants – a blow to the many catering and hospitality firms who had come on board.

Blazing sunshine graced the proceedings and the crowd was very vocal in support of Britain's great hope, the aforementioned Barry Hoban. Despite the encouragement though he could only manage ninth place in the Plymouth stage and the yellow jersey was won by that year's youngest entrant, 21-year-old Dutchman Henk Poppe, who was in his first full season as a professional.

Henk didn't hold on to the coveted covering for long as the eventual winner proved to be one of the sport's true legends, Belgium's Eddy Merckx, whose success in 1974 saw him equal Jacques Anquetil's record of five Tour de France victories.

Reckoned to be one of cycling's greatest ever figures, Eddy went on to win further titles in 1975, 1976 and 1977.

This page and opposite: *The Tour de France comes to Plymouth and the A38.*

It wasn't just cyclists being forced to be more safety conscious in the Seventies, car drivers too, especially those involved with rallies, races and hill climbs, like the Plymouth Motor Club, were having to reappraise their approach to a variety of issues, such as: the number of marshals required at events; whether there was still an audience for autocross; whether rallies starting and/or ending on the Hoe were still acceptable to the local authorities and, indeed, to the main motoring organisations ... and whether it was still feasible, or even financially viable, to allow spectators at hill climbs.

An RAC official argued that it would be prohibitively expensive to fence spectators in while another said it was imperative for the PMC to have an ambulance in attendance. A decision was made to open discussions with St John Ambulance officials.

Meanwhile, Hemerdon was a popular hill climb venue and PMC's 1972 event there attracted over 50 entries. Local driver and garage proprietor, Chris Inch, put in the best performance of the day.

Treasure Hunts, meanwhile, which had become increasingly popular with the spread of car ownership, were another cause for concern.

Opposite page: *1971, A Triumph Rally on Plymouth Hoe.* Top right: *1977, Plymouth stages rally, a Ford Escort takes a bend at speed.* Above left: *1970. Mrs. June Gould with some of the family silverware* Bottom right: *Harry (driver) and Neil (navigator) Gould on Guy Fawkes Rally in the South Hams, November 1972.*

If the roads were becoming busier, so to were the waterways. Plymouth was boasting two yacht clubs — the Royal Western Yacht Club of England, based at West Hoe, and the Royal Plymouth Corinthian Yacht CLub, off Madeira Road, below the Citadel. Both were established in the nineteenth century. There were also a number of sailing clubs: West Hoe; Torpoint Mosquito, Carew Wharf, Torpoint; Tamar River Club, at Saltash Passage; Plym Yacht Club at Oreston and the Mayflower Sailing Club at Commercial Wharf, as well as one or two other peripheral clubs, at Newton Ferrers and Bere Alston.

For those not involved in clubs there were two main dinghy parks with slipways that could be used at any state of the tide; at Elphinstone, by the Mayflower Club, and at Queen Anne Battery on the other side of the entrance to Sutton Harbour. Other slipway facilities were available at Richmond Walk, Oreston and Saltash Passage.

Richmond Walk and Sutton Harbour were also where the two new pontoon mooring arrangements were offering 'comprehensive services for ocean-going and cruising yachtsmen'.

Additional harbour facilities were available at Millbay which were managed by the Boatswain of the Royal Western Yacht Club. Potential visitors were advised that showers, fresh water and fuel were all available at Millbay, while the nearest source of supplies and provisions was the Post Office/Newsagents at West Hoe.

Opposite page: *July 1973, Queen Anne Battery slipway.*
Top and bottom right: *Elphinstone slipway.* Above: *Sailing in the Cattewater.*

235

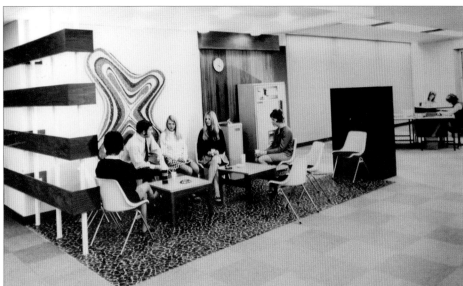

This page: *Various shots of the new SWEB offices at Manadon, in 1972, including, top left, Jill Demelweek and Carol Kellaway at their desks with state-of-the-art VDUs. Bottom right: A young lady working at a filing/retrieval system, possibly made at Remington Rand and called a Lektriever.*

WORKING LIFE

One of the most interesting, and, undoubtedly, one of the most state-of-the-art workplaces to open in the Seventies in Plymouth was the new South Western Electricity Board building just off Manadon Roundabout, at the end of Outland Road.

The new £900,000 accounting offices included £1 million-worth of 'complex computer equipment'. Two-thirds of its 350-plus staff were women and, interestingly enough, although it was acceptable for the women to be married, they couldn't be mothers — and there was no question of maternity pay. Nevertheless, it was somehow fitting that the building was opened by only the second ever woman to wear Plymouth's mayoral chains, Dorothy Innes.

February 1972 when the building commenced operations, incidentally, was a strange time for SWEB. At the time there were concerns about potential power cuts to save fuel which was in short supply because of the coal strike, and SWEB had to publish disconnection rotas in the morning and evening papers on Thursdays, and in most weekly papers appearing that week.

Above: *The new, in 1972, SWEB offices in Outland Road, at Manadon.*

Clockwise from top left: *The Vi-Spring plant at Ernesettle; craftsmen at work, the hand-made process a key part of the Vi Spring offer; One of the Vi-Spring Bedford lorries.*

SWEB had been operating out of offices in the City Centre before moving to Manadon. By contrast, Vi-Spring had been operating out of a factory in London prior to 1971, although, admittedly there had been a mattress making business on the edge of the Tamar at Ernesettle since Slumberland had taken on the Clattworthy company in 1957.

Vi-Spring had been bought out by Slumberland a few years earlier. Subsequently the bigger company had used the opportunity to exploit the premium hand-manufactured brand that Vi-Spring were famous for. They mechanised, modernised and mass-produced mattresses, using new and synthetic materials along the way.

The new product was not nearly as expensive but the retailers hated it. Many refused to stock it. The fallout over the fiasco cost the company around £750,000, a massive amount. Vi-Spring's new parent company decided to cut their losses and sell the Willesden plant where Vi-Spring had been making mattresses since 1915.

It was a blow to many of the men who worked there, including members of the management who felt betrayed by the move into mass production and they asked if they could have the Vi-Spring name and relocate to another of the parent company's plants, the Slumberland factory in Plymouth.

Thus it was that one of Britain's premium brands came to take up residence in Plymouth, exactly 70 years after their revolutionary six-spring-pocket approach to bedding had transformed the surfaces we all sleep on.

Above: *Traditional tools, traditional materials.*

With the national unemployment rate in the mid-Seventies running at around 6.1%, Plymouth was particularly grateful for any employment-generating openings. The unemployment rate here was running much higher, at 9%. Ever since the war there had been efforts and incentives to bring major employers to the area. In the Seventies, following the Government's decision to make Plymouth an 'Intermediate Area' to encourage industrial growth, it meant that manufacturers establishing factories in the City could claim 20% Regional Development Grants towards the cost of factory building, as well as other financial assistance and a full range of Development Area training grants.

Furthermore there were also industrial development certificates readily available, whereby the Department of Industry would, in suitable situations, build factories for companies who preferred to operate out of rented accommodation, rather than build their own premises.

All in all, by the mid-Seventies around 50 new factories had been built and some 14,000 people gainfully employed. Foremost among those that arrived in the Seventies were the chewing-gum giant from Chicago — Wrigleys.

Building on a green-field site at Estover they set up their only European base, in Plymouth, at the beginning of the decade. A couple of years later they introduced their first new product lines in a very long time — Freedent — *'the gum that will not stick to most dental work'* and Big Red, a cinnamon-flavoured gum that was a sister-gum to Juicy Fruit, the companies flagship flavour, which, like Spearmint, had been first introduced to the undersides of unsuspecting school desks in 1893.

Other American, or American-controlled companies who had opted to establish post-war Plymouth outposts included: Acheson Colloids, Aulecon Electronics, the Barden Corporation, Bellows International, Brown & Sharpe, Fine Tubes, Gleasons, the Paper Converting Machine Company, Ranco Controls, Stafford Miller Limited and Texas Instruments.

Meanwhile, amongst the homegrown manufacturers and those from this side of the Atlantic, were: AD International, Alderman Tooling, Aqueous Systems, Arrow Hart, George Becs Toolmaker (who like Bill Aldernman was an ex-Tecalemit man), Berker Sportcraft, printers Clarke, Doble & Brendon, Clarks shoes, Robert Daniel's Cash and Carry business, David Pneumatics, Edmund Metal Works, Electroloid, Glaxo Farley, Gardiner Refrigeration, FE Harris, Hatfield Instruments, Jaeger, Anthony Jennings Clothing, Ladybird, LSI (Electronic Systems), Plessey, McArthur Steel & Plastics, ML Engineering, Marine Projects, Owen (Clothing), Plymouth Cold Stores, Plymouth Glass, Plymouth Portable Buildings, Pyropress, Rank Radio, Renwicks, DF Rowe, Smedley Food Group, Smith's Food Group, Sperry Gyroscope, Tecalemit, Uglow's Bakery, Westward Building, Westwood Engineering, Whateley & Co, and E Whiteland Engineering.

Top: Wrigley's Factory n 1979. Middle: Other Estover plants. Bottom: A Merryweather fire engine in Tecalemit's interior plating shop. Opposite page: The huge Tecalemit complex at Marsh Mills, 1979.

Even a lot of the non-American businesses though were non-Plymouth concerns, indeed it was said that 40% of the manufacturing firms in the City were subsidiaries of larger companies and there are, of course, almost invariably downsides to the presence of non-indigenous companies. They tend to make fewer purchases in the local area, profits are not always reinvested locally and decisions are often made externally that massively impact on local economy without that ever being a consideration for the decision makers.

It wasn't always an easy ride for the local factories either however, and one that struggled through the Seventies was Berketex. The well-known clothing firm had arrived in Plymouth in the Fifties, in the first wave of post-war industrial development, but as the availability of cheap imports increased so it became harder to compete and survive.

The largest dressmaking factory in Europe at one point, with a 1,500 strong workforce, that figure had reduced to around 60 by 1970 and closure looked inevitable, but four managers stepped in to save the company.

Improvements followed and they even started recruiting again. Manager Freddie Ballantine introduced a crèche facility, one of the first in the City, whereby the women workers could bring their children in in the morning and collect them at the end of their shift. At one point they had up to 40 children there.

Incidentally, most children born in the Seventies arrived in one of three maternity homes in the City; Freedom Fields, the Alexander Maternity Home and at Devonport Maternity Home.

The days of both were numbered, however, once work had begun on the first phase of the 'space-age' new hospital at Derriford, in 1974.

Built at a cost of an estimated £22 million, the work involved the creation of a building that was a massive 52,000 square metres in size.

A site engineer claimed that the place would make Freedom Fields look like a cottage hospital. However by the end of the decade the job was still a work in progress and no patients had been admitted.

Rather, the City's hospital facilities were spread across a number of sites: Freedom Fields and Greenbank, Lockyer Street, Royal Albert (Devonport) and the Royal Naval Hospital in Stonehouse. Supporting roles were played by Scott Hospital, Mount Gould, the Royal Eye Infirmary, Crownhill Convalescent Home, Plympton Hospital and the Gables (also at Plympton), and Wolseley Home. There was also the Chest Clinic at Beaumont House, a Physiotherapy Department in Dale Road and a general Health Centre at Plympton.

Visiting times were 'liberal' and generally controlled by the sisters in charge of the wards.

Top: *Break-time at Bush Radio.* Bottom: *Berketex cutting room.*

September 1975 work in progress on the new Derriford Hospital.

Inset top: *Early-Seventies inspection at Mount Batten.* Above: *The Mount Batten Peninsula.*

FOR QUEEN AND COUNTRY

Plymouth's proud, and perhaps, unique record of having all four of the armed services represented within area, since the fourth branch, the Royal Naval Air Service (RAF), had come into existence during the Great War, was still in place as the Seventies dawned.

Admittedly the general defence presence had dwindled, nationally as well as locally — although nationally the spending on defence was fairly constant throughout the decade, at around 4.5% of the GDP (Gross Domestic Product).

Nevertheless, Plumer Barracks had disappeared altogether, Raglan, apart from its fine gatehouse, had been swept away and RAF Mount Batten had struggled for an identity ever since the Australian Flying Boat Squadron had left at the end of the Second World War. A Marine Craft Training School for a while, then the base of the RAF Marine Branch from 1961, Mount Batten was far from being somewhere with a great future.

The Royal Citadel upon the Hoe, by contrast, as well as having a past that stretched back 300 years, still appeared in good health as one of the oldest fortifications in continuous military occupation in the western world.

Apart from a few hockey players and the odd occasion when it was opened up for shows and spectaculars ... and the odd guided tour, few people were afforded the opportunity to see inside the walls.

Above: *28 January 1971 RAF Mount Batten play RAF Hullavington in a cup match.*

Life inside the Royal Citadel had changed a little back in 1962, when 29 Commando Light Regiment Royal Artillery arrived and the base had become the home of the Commando Gunners.

For the rest of the Sixties and into the Seventies one or other of the two Commando Regiments were based here, and then, in 1976, the two merged as one and became 29 Commando Regiment Royal Artillery, and the Citadel became their Headquarters.

In the Sixties and early Seventies the Commando Gunners served in support of 3 Commando Brigade Royal Marines in various operations around the world, notably in the Middle East and the Far East.

Meanwhile, the eighteenth-century Royal Marine Barracks at Stonehouse soldiered on, little changed throughout the Seventies, while the major alterations to the Royal Naval Dockyard have been covered earlier in this book.

Top: *General Officer Commanding Sir Frank King visits 29 Commando and the Citadel, 1972.*

Bottom left and right: *Inside the Citadel.* Inset right: *Queen's Birthday Salute, from Citadel, 1971.*

The main, other area of expansion in the Armed Service offer in the City at this time, was perhaps not surprisingly one of the newest of the facilities, the Royal Naval Engineering College at Manadon.

The 100-acre site at Manadon had been in use by the Navy, as an engineering college, since 1940, when it had been housed mainly in a series of temporary buildings.

The instructional block and factory buildings were completed in 1951 and five years later Earl Mountbatten laid the foundation stone of a new accommodation block and wardroom.

Further accommodation, a large lecture theatre-cum-cinema, new sports facilities and a converted chapel (created inside a seventeenth-century tithe barn) saw the Royal Naval Engineering College transformed into something that was doubtless akin to what Lieutenant Robert Wall had anticipated back in 1831, when he published his somewhat visionary *Suggestions for the Establishment of a Naval University with some observations on the formation of a Corps of Naval Engineers.*

Of course that had almost been at the dawn of the Industrial Revolution, when the Royal Navy was still heavily reliant on sail rather than steam. Furthermore, there's no way that Wall could have envisaged the sort of technology and sophisticated engineering that was being used by the Royal Navy in the Seventies, but doubtless he would have been impressed by Manadon.

With its excellent educational and research facilities, it clearly differed from most other degree-awarding institutions in that its successful students, also being officers in training, were guaranteed work after graduation. They were also required to wear uniform, and to attend lectures, but what other establishment offered the chance that the Queen may consent to come down to present the annual academic awards as she was to do in the early Eighties?

It's doubtless on account of the City's reputation as a base for the Armed Services that Plymouth has, historically, been well blessed with royal visitations. The Duke of Edinburgh has been a particularly frequent visitor, his office as Lord High Steward of Plymouth almost certainly having a bearing on that.

The Duke of Edinburgh visits RNEC Manadon, 1970.

247

In the Seventies alone, the Duke was here in July 1970 visiting the *Kathleen & May* and the Tall Ships race; the following year he was back on 13 November being greeted at North Road Station by the Lord Mayor, Dorothy Innes. She was also on hand, three days later, on 16 November 1971, to receive Princess Anne when she came to officially open the new Mayflower Sports Centre and Drake Circus shopping complex.

Meanwhile, an even greater occasion ushered in the Duke's next visit, with the Queen, as part of Her Majesty's Silver Jubilee Celebrations on 5 August 1977. Thousands lined the streets and packed the Guildhall Square. Council Staff were given an extra day off. A truly festive spirit swept across the City and 6 June saw a number of Silver Jubilee street parties across the City and up and down the country.

All in all the Queen spent three months on the road visiting various towns, cities and countries. Indeed together with the Duke of Edinburgh she visited more places in Britain than any previous monarch in such a short space of time — and, even more impressively, they visited some 36 different countries.

Top left: *The Queen at St Andrew's with John Watson and Mike and Judy Veale.*
Middle: *The Queen and Prince Philip with the Lord Mayor, Arthur Floyd and his wife.*
Bottom: *Princess Anne visits the new Tesco store in Drake Circus, 1971.*
Above: *My Jubilee cartoon.*

June 1977, Fullerton Road Jubilee celebration street party, Milehouse.

Plymouth's Lord Mayors of the Seventies

1969-70   George Ernest Hillyer Creber
1970-71   Eric Donald Nuttall
1971-72   Mrs Dorothy FW Innes
1972-73   Jack Lester Luce
1973-74   John Clifford Porter
1974-75   George Ernest Hillyer Creber
1975-76   Frederick William Johnson
1976-77   William Ivor Thompson
1977-78   Arthur Raymond Floyd
1978-79   Robert Ramsey Thornton
1979-80   William Evan Evans

Lord Mayor, Dorothy Innes and The Duke of Edinburgh.

Plymouth's MPs of the Seventies

1970 Dame Joan Vickers, Devonport (C)
       David Owen, Sutton (L)

1974 David Owen, Devonport (L)
       Hon. Alan Clark, Sutton (C)
       Janet Fookes, Drake (C)

1974 David Owen, Devonport (L)
       Hon. Alan Clark, Sutton (C)
       Janet Fookes, Drake (C)

1979 David Owen, Devonport (L)
       Hon. Alan Clark, Sutton (C)
       Janet Fookes, Drake (C)

Clockwise from top left: David Owen, Dame Joan Vickers, Alan Clark, and Janet Fookes.

ACKNOWLEDGEMENTS

Many of the images that appear in this book have been supplied by readers of my 'Looking Back' column in the *Herald*. In some instances they were photographs that had originally been taken for the paper back in the Seventies, but in others they are simply happy snaps that have captured the essence of the era. These wonderfully evocative shots were, more often than not, unplanned and unposed, and yet they have a magical quality which adds much to this review. The archives of the *Herald* and *Western Morning News* have also been immensely useful. Thanks go to Alan Cooper, Alan Qualtrough, Bill Martin and Paul Burton. The bulk of this material is now curated by the Plymouth Barbican Trust's South West Image Bank at 25 Parade, on the Barbican — thanks there go to the Directors, the volunteers and the SWIB archivist Colette Hobbs.

The Plymouth Central Library Local Studies Department and the Plymouth City Museum and Art Gallery have also been very helpful. So too have old books, tourist guides, brochures, and souvenir programmes.

From a practical and personal perspective, I'd also like to express very grateful thanks to my publisher Clare (who is also my best friend and long-suffering wife), mother-in-law Patricia Greathead, long-term friend and New Street colleague, Rob Warren, former Latimer Trend man Bill Bugler, who also proof read our first ever book 30 years ago, Mike and Anne Corry and Beverley Kinsella, all of whom have read this looking for typos and other irritants.

I'd also like to say a special thank you to number two son, Ben Robinson, who wasn't even a twinkle in the Seventies and who has painstakingly gone through this book making sure all the photographs were the right size, in the right format and in the right position.

Thanks too to Latimer Trend, who have printed all our books, bar one, over the last 30 years and who have always been a joy to deal with: that's particularly to Paul Opie, Dave Manners, Andrew Denham and Sharon Bell, who are ever at the frontline.

Top: *Last year at school, in the art room with my mother, 1973.*
Middle: *Broad Park Road, May 1975, hire car driven down from Leeds.*
Bottom: *My first drawing of the Hoe, 1972.*

Meanwhile, the A-Z list of those individuals who have sent me photographs over the last thirty years or so — photographs that have helped make this book what it is — is once again a very long one, I only hope I haven't left anyone out!

But even before I mention anyone else I need to say a big thank you to Bernard Mills, Derek Tait, Stephen Johnson (Cyberheritage), Ed Sijmons, Tony Byers, Roy Westlake, Bernard Mills, Roy Perring, Keith Jenkin, Brian Bailey, and Keith Loze, for permission to use their excellent photographic images and archives.

With thanks to: Mick Adams, Roger Arborfield, Francis Baker, Phil Barrow, Victor Barton, Ian Bickle, Tony Benwell, Robin Blythe-Lord, Margaret Bond, John and Sylvia Boulden, Tom Bowden, Graham and Pat Brooks, Jean Brown, Paul Burtnyk, Peter Carlyle, Derek Carter, Robert Cattrall, Tim Charlesworth, Jean Chapman, Peter Coleman, Bob Cook, Mike Cox, Harvey Crane, Bernice Dann, Maurice Dart, Ralph Delbridge, Andy Endacott, Marilyn Endacott, Dennis Escott, Guy Fleming, Sylvia Franklin, Daryle Gay, Crispin Gill, Duncan Godefroy, Keith Gorman, Jim Griffin, Terry Guswell, Fred Guy, Vincent Hart, Hatti Hayne, Barry Henderson, Ron Hellyer, Derek Hiscock, Graham Hobbins, Barbara Horner, Andy Howard, Pete Isbell, Mike Hocking, Dot Inch, John James, Daryl Jago, David Jennings, Ron Johns, David King, Alan Kittridge, Mary and Gerald Knight, Harley Lawer, Trevor Lear, Alan and Annette Lemin, Graham Little, Mike Luxton, Ray McSweeny, Ray Mitchell, Brian Moseley, Frank Moulder, Sid Oliver, Pete Organ, Cynthia Palmer, Richard and Jane Palmer, Mike Parriss, May Parson, Alan Pease, Joe Pengelly, Jean Perkins, John Pinch, Frank Pocock, Merv Pollard, Richard Score, Charlie Sells, Dave Sharp, Gordon Sparks, Jeanette Simpson, Reg Smith, Len Stevens, Peter Taylor, David Tozer, Gerry Tucker, Don Tucker, John Walters, Jimmy Warren, Rob Warren, Peter Warrren, Jim Warwick, Gerald Wasley, Peter Waterhouse, Tony Way, Mike White, Peter Williamson, Mary Wills, Jonathan Wood, Sonia Wright, and Mike Yeats.

While every care has been taken to try and identify individual copyright holders the publishers would be happy to hear from anyone who has information concerning the copyright of any uncredited images.

Chris Robinson *November 2015*

Right top: *Des, Brenda, Clare and Chris Robinson, Plymouth Hoe, 1978.*
Middle: *With Clare in Broad Park Road, Peverell, in the snow, late-Seventies.*
Bottom left: *Derek Tait on a space hopper. in St Budeaux.*
Right: *Seventies art college student, and Cyberheritage man, Stephen Johnson..*

BIBLIOGRAPHY

  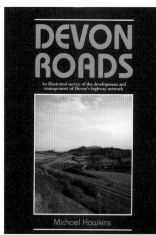 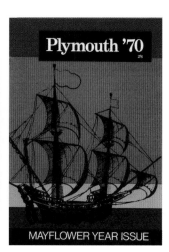

A Century of Plymouth: Events, People and Places over the last 100 years – **Guy Fleming**, Sutton Publishing Ltd (2000)

A 1970s Childhood: From Glam Rock to Happy Days – **Derek Tait,** (2011)

A Torch In Flame: The History of Devonport High School for Boys – **Henry Whitfeld**, Devon Books (1987)

The Argyle Book – **Terry Guswell & Chris Robinson,** Pen & Ink (2002)

Argyle Classics – **Harley Lawer,** Green Books, Plymouth (1988)

Backtracking Around Friary, Laira and the Plym – **Bernard Mills,** Pen & Ink Publishing (2013)

Britain in the Seventies – **Ronald Allison,** Country Life Books (1980)

Citadel: A History of the Royal Citadel, Plymouth – **Freddie Woodward,** Devon Books (1987)

Dear Fatty – **Dawn French,** Century (2008)

Devon at the Cinema: An Illustrated History of Cinema Going – **Gordon Chapman**, Devon Books (2000)

Devon Roads – **Michael Hawkins,** Devon Books (1988)

Devonport Dockyard Railway – **Paul Burkhalter,** Twelveheads Press (1996)

Devonport Dockyard Story – **Lt-Cdr Ken Burns,** Maritime Books (1984)

Elizabethan Plymouth – **Chris Robinson**, Pen & Ink (2002)

Fleet History of Plymouth Corporation and Plymouth Citybus Limited – The P.S.V

A History of Devonport – **Chris Robinson,** Pen & Ink (2010)

Images of Plymouth – **Tom Bowden,** Sutton Publishing (2006)

Images of England: Plymouth – **Derek Tait**, Tempus Publishing Ltd (2003)

The Making of the University of Plymouth – **Alston Kennerley**, University of Plymouth

Naval Heritage in The West: Part I, II & III – **Andy Endacott** (1986, 1987, 1988)

Notes on the Barbican Mural – **Robert O Lenkiewicz,** Ferns Publishing (1972)

150 Years of the Co-operative in Plymouth – **Chris Robinson,** Pen & Ink (2009)

Playbill: A History of Theatre in the Westcountry – **Harvey Crane,** Macdonald & Evans Ltd (1980)

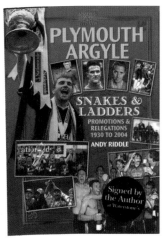  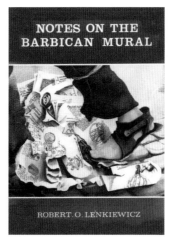  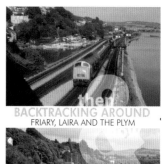

Plymouth Argyle: The Complete Record – **Ryan Danes,** Breedon Books (2009)
Plymouth Argyle: The Modern Era – **Andy Riddle,** Desert Island Books (2002)
Plymouth Argyle: Snakes & Ladders – **Andy Riddle,** Desert Isand Books (2004)
Plymouth: A New History – **Crispin Gill,** Devon Books (1993)
Plymouth: As Time Draws On Vols 1 & 2 – **Chris Robinson,** Pen & Ink Publishing (1985, 1988)
Plymouth Cricket Club 1857-2007 – **Phil Barrow,** Plymouth CC (2007)
Plymouth: Maritime City in Transition – **Brian Chalkley, David Dunkerley, Peter Gripaios,** David & Charles (1991)
Plymouth: Official Guide – The Entertainments and Publicity Department of the City Council, Underhill Ltd (1969-78)
Plymouth: Pictures from the Past – **Guy Fleming,** The Devonshire Press Ltd (1995)
Plymouth Vision of a Modern City – **Jeremy Gould,** English Heritage (2010)
Plymouth Yesterday Today – **Vic Saundercock** (1989)
Plymouth's Historic Barbican – **Chris Robinson,** Pen & Ink Publishing (2007)
Royal Visits to Devon and Cornwall: Images from the WMN and Evening Herald 1900-2000 – **John Van Der Kiste,** Halsgrove (2002)
Scouting in Plymouth 1908 - 1982 – **Graham E. Brooks and Arthur L. Clamp,** P.D.S. Printers Ltd (1982)
Tamar High School: The Best of the Past – **Ray Rose,** Ray Rose (1996)
The 75th Anniversary Book of Plymouth Civil Service Sports & Leisure Club – **Ron Cook,** Mirro Image (2002)
Ships in Plymouth Sound – **Sydney Goodman,** Halsgrove (1999)
Steam Around Plymouth – **Bernard Mills,** Tempus Publishing Ltd (2003)
Sutton Harbour – **Crispin Gill,** Devon Books (1997)
Union Street – **Chris Robinson,** Pen & Ink (2000)
Victorian Plymouth: As Time Draws On – **Chris Robinson,** Pen & Ink Publishing (1991)
Vi-Spring: Over a century of Luxurious Sleep – **Chris Robinson,** Pen & Ink Publishing (2013)
West Park Remembered: 1930-1970 – **Derry Purvis,** Pen & Ink Publishing (2013)

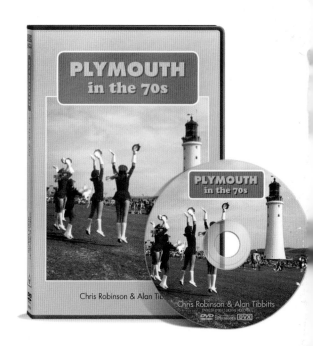

   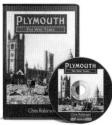